IS GOD REAL?

FOR TEENS

Also by Lee Strobel

The Case for Christ
The Case for Christ Student Edition (with Jane Vogel)
The Case for Christ curriculum (with Garry Poole)
The Case for Christ Devotional (with Mark Mittelberg)
The Case for Christ audio
The Case for Christ for Kids (with Rob Suggs and Robert Elmer)
The Case for a Creator
The Case for a Creator Student Edition (with Jane Vogel)
The Case for a Creator curriculum (with Garry Poole)
The Case for a Creator audio
The Case for a Creator for Kids (with Rob Suggs and Robert Elmer)
The Case for Faith
The Case for Faith Student Edition (with Jane Vogel)
The Case for Faith curriculum (with Garry Poole)
The Case for Faith audio
The Case for Faith for Kids (with Rob Suggs and Robert Elmer)
The Case for Grace
The Case for Grace Student Edition (with Jane Vogel)
The Case for Grace for Kids (with Jesse Florea)
The Case for Miracles
The Case for Miracles Student Edition (with Jane Vogel)
The Case for Miracles for Kids (with Jesse Florea)
The Case for Christmas
The Case for Easter
The Case for Heaven
God's Outrageous Claims
In Defense of Jesus
Is God Real?
Seeing the Supernatural
Spiritual Mismatch (with Leslie Strobel)
Today's Moment of Truth (with Mark Mittelberg)
The Unexpected Adventure (with Mark Mittelberg)

ZONDERVAN

Is God Real? For Teens

Published in Grand Rapids, Michigan, by Zondervan. Zondervan is a registered trademark of The Zondervan Corporation, L.L.C., a wholly owned subsidiary of HarperCollins Christian Publishing, Inc.

Requests for information should be addressed to customercare@harpercollins.com.

ISBN 978-0-310-17985-6 (hardcover)

In Chapter 1, the quotation from Kai Nielsen is from *Reason and Practice: A Modern Introduction to Philosophy* (New York: Harper & Row, 1971), 48. The Quentin Smith quotation is from William Lane Craig and Quentin Smith, *Theism, Atheism, and Big Bang Cosmology* (Oxford, UK: Clarendon Press, 1993), 135. The Timothy Ferris quote is from *The Whole Shebang: A State-of-the-Universe(s) Report* (New York: Touchstone, 1998), 265.

In Chapter 4, quotations from Polycarp are from his "Letter to the Philippians," 9:2, translation by Gary Habermas and Michael R. Licona. The Tryggve N. D. Mettinger quotations are from *The Riddle of Resurrection: "Dying and Rising Gods" in the Ancient Near East* (Stockholm: Almqvist & Wicksell, 2001), 221.

In Chapter 8, the baseball story is from Kenneth Samples, "Divine Hiddenness: A Sender or Receiver Problem?" in *Worldview Bulletin*, December 30, 2022.

In the Conclusion, the John Lennox quote is from a video posted on his website and titled "Is It Reasonable to Believe in God?", dated June 4, 2020, accessed April 3, 2025, https://www.johnlennox.org/resources/175/is-it-reasonable-to-believe.

Italics in Scripture quotations are the author's emphasis.

Author is represented by the literary agent Don Gates at The Gates Group, www.the-gates-group.com.

HarperCollins Publishers, Macken House, 39/40 Mayor Street Upper, Dublin 1, D01 C9W8, Ireland (https://www.harpercollins.com)

Library of Congress Cataloging-in-Publication Data

ISBN 978-0-310-17985-6

Printed in the United States of America

26 27 28 29 30 LBC 7 6 5 4 3

IS GOD REAL? FOR TEENS

EXPLORING FAITH *in a* WORLD OF WONDER

LEE STROBEL

Believing in something doesn't make it true.
Hoping that something is true doesn't make it true.
The existence of God is not subjective.
He either exists or he doesn't.
It's not a matter of opinion.
You can have your own opinions.
But you can't have your own facts.

—British actor and writer Ricky Gervais,
"Why I'm an Atheist,"
Wall Street Journal, December 9, 2010

CONTENTS

INTRODUCTION

How My Search Began

My spiritual doubts began when I was a teenager.

I'd been raised by parents who were Christians, but my own beliefs were shallow. Then in middle school I began asking uncomfortable questions, such as why a loving God would allow suffering. Nobody seemed willing to engage with me. I figured that was because there were no good answers.

In high school I was taught that evolution explained the origin and diversity of life, so God was out of a job. It seemed like I needed to make a choice between science or religion—and I chose the empirical over the theological.

When I was a freshman in college, I took a course on the historical Jesus that was taught by a skeptic. He convinced me that history can't tell us anything reliable about the resurrection.

By then, atheism had firmly taken root within me. And when I embarked on my career as a cynical journalist at one of America's largest newspapers, my atheism continued to deepen.

That is, until my agnostic wife became a Christian. Hoping to liberate her from this cult, I decided to use my journalism and legal training to investigate the truth about Christianity. Though I hoped I could debunk the faith, I was nevertheless determined to do a fair and thorough exploration of the biggest question of life: *Is God real?*

As for you, I'm so glad you're checking out this life-changing and eternity-altering topic. Whether you're a doubter like I was, or a confident Christian looking for further affirmation of your faith, I hope my book will provide evidence to satisfy your heart and soul.

Remember that God doesn't get angry at us when we express our hesitations about him. When John the Baptist was thrown into prison and began to question the identity of Jesus, he sent friends to ask Jesus whether he really was the long-awaited Messiah.

How did Jesus respond? Did he get angry that John (of all people!) dared to ask such a question? No. We can read in Luke 7 how he instructed those friends to go back and tell John what they had seen with their own eyes. And what they had seen was evidence that he is who he claimed to be: the unique, miracle-working Son of God.

Let me assure you that it's fine to ask questions about God. It's permissible to wrestle with objections to Christianity. It's even okay to have doubts—as long as you do what John did by pursuing solid answers.

As this book will show, there are indeed good scientific, historical, and philosophical reasons to conclude that Christianity is true. There are even sufficient responses to the toughest challenges to the faith.

Regardless of your religious perspective, I hope you'll read these pages with an open mind and receptive heart. Jesus said (in Matthew 7:7) that if you seek, you'll find. So seek with confidence and curiosity and courage.

Determine where the evidence points. I hope you'll then take a step of faith in the same direction. That's logical. That's rational. We do that every day of our life in a variety of circumstances.

Except this time, the stakes are higher than ever.

I'll be cheering you on!

Christianity is true. There are even sufficient responses to the toughest challenges to the faith.

Regardless of your religious perspective, I hope you'll read these pages with an open mind and receptive heart. [illegible] [illegible] them. [illegible] if you seek, you'll find [illegible] with confidence and curiosity and courage.

Determine where the evidence points, then take a step of faith in the same direction. That's logical. That's rational. [illegible] that every day of our life [illegible] [illegible].

Except this time, the stakes are higher than ever.

I'll be cheering you on.

CHAPTER 1

THE COSMOS REQUIRES A CREATOR

I'm guessing you've done this before. You found yourself staring upward into a star-filled sky, or maybe at distant mountaintops or forests or the ocean. And you began to wonder.

Where did everything come from?

Thousands of years ago, the Hebrews believed they had the answer. The Bible opens with these words: "In the beginning God created the heavens and the earth." It quickly goes on to claim that everything began just with God's voice ordering light into existence.

What's your view of this claim? Too simple? Superstitious? Maybe a made-up myth?

Or could it be an insight that's supernaturally inspired? Could the beginning of our universe actually point toward the existence of a divine creator?

Perhaps that conclusion isn't really necessary. Early in this century, a bestselling book was published that explored all kinds of science on an easy-to-understand level. It was titled *A Short History of Nearly Everything.* And on page 13, author Bill Bryson suggested that the existence of the universe is self-explanatory. "It seems impossible that you could get something from nothing," he wrote, "but the fact that once there was nothing, and now there is a universe, is evident proof that you can."

Could this be the whole story? Or does that explanation leave your mind wanting more?

My mind wants more. And that desire sent me to an Atlanta suburb to interview an expert who has studied and debated these issues for decades.

Something Called Kalam

William Lane Craig is a university professor of philosophy who has been named one of the fifty most influential philosophers alive today. He has two doctoral degrees, and he's spoken at major universities around the world, including Harvard, Yale, Stanford, Oxford, Cambridge, and Moscow. As an author, he has more than thirty books to his credit, plus more than a hundred articles in professional journals of philosophy and theology.

As we talked, I found Bill Craig to be highly skilled in communicating complex concepts in understandable and yet technically accurate language.

He and I talked first about something called "the kalam cosmological argument for God's existence." Dr. Craig is famous for supporting this idea, and he gave me the historical background for it.

In ancient Greece, he told me, Aristotle had believed that God wasn't the creator of the universe, but simply supplied the universe with order. In Aristotle's view, as Craig explained, "both God and the universe are eternal. Of course, that contradicted the Hebrew notion that God created the world out of nothing. So Christians later sought to refute Aristotle."

Later, when the Muslim religion took over North Africa, Muslim theologians picked up these arguments because they also believed in creation. Over time, the word *kalam*—which is Arabic for "speech" or "doctrine"—was used in the Middle Ages for the whole thrust of Muslim theology. It included a "cosmological argument" with three simple steps:

1. Whatever begins to exist has a cause.
2. The universe began to exist.
3. Therefore, the universe has a cause.

Our discussion made its way through all three steps.

Step 1: Whatever Begins to Exist Has a Cause

Craig told me that when he first began defending this kalam argument, he expected this first statement to be accepted by virtually everyone. He expected the second premise—that the universe began to exist—to be much more controversial. But he said that as more and more scientific evidence supports the idea that the universe had a beginning, atheists have been forced to attack any supposed *cause* behind it.

"This is absolutely bewildering!" Craig said, shaking his head. "Things don't just pop into existence, uncaused, out of nothing."

But not everyone agrees. Craig once coauthored a book with atheist philosopher Quentin Smith. Their book was a back-and-forth debate on the issues of theism, atheism, and the Big Bang theory. He said Quentin Smith concluded his part of the book with this claim: "The most reasonable belief is that we came from nothing, by nothing, and for nothing."

People who don't accept the idea of a cause behind every beginning are generally unable to offer evidence for their position, Craig noted. "Instead, they fold their arms and play the skeptic by saying, 'You can't prove that's true.' They dial their degree of skepticism so high that nothing could possibly convince them."

So I asked Craig what positive proof he could offer for saying that whatever begins to exist has a cause.

He answered, "This is intuitively obvious once you clearly grasp the concept of absolute nothingness. You see, the idea that things can come into being uncaused out of *nothing* is worse than magic. At least when a magician pulls a rabbit out of a hat, there's the magician and the hat! But in atheism, the universe just pops into being out of nothing, with absolutely no explanation at all."

People who don't accept the idea of a cause behind every beginning are generally unable to offer evidence for their position. "Instead, they fold their arms and play the skeptic by saying, 'You can't prove that's true.' They dial their degree of skepticism so high that nothing could possibly convince them."

What Craig was saying seemed hard to dispute. But I wanted to know what scientific evidence he could give.

He said that in reality this principle has been constantly proved all around us and has never been shown to be false. "We never see things coming into being uncaused out of nothing. Nobody worries that while they're away at work, say, a horse might pop into being in their living room—uncaused, out of nothing—and stand there ruining the carpet. We don't worry about those kinds of things because they never happen. So this is a principle that is constantly verified by science."

But then I remembered a potentially huge objection to this reasoning. In the wacky world of quantum physics, all kinds of strange, unexpected things happen at the subatomic level. And that's the level where the entire universe existed in its very earliest stages—back when electrons, protons, and neutrinos were bursting forth in the so-called Big Bang. This "quantum weirdness" was a place where, as science writer Timothy Ferris put it, "the logical foundations of classical science are violated." Could it be that our common-sense notions of cause and effect just don't apply here?

I told Craig about a magazine article which said that according to quantum theory, things *can* materialize out of a vacuum—even though it's generally only pairs of subatomic particles with short lives. To generate something as large as a molecule was considered "profoundly unlikely." Yet as far back as fifty years ago, scientists had suggested that the entire universe might have come into existence in this way.

Craig informed me that the subatomic particles the article

talks about are called "virtual particles." They're theoretical, he said, and it isn't clear that they actually exist.

"However," he added, "there's a much more important point here. You see, these particles—if they are real—do *not* come out of nothing. The quantum vacuum is not what most people envision when they think of a vacuum—that is, *absolutely* nothing. On the contrary, it's a sea of fluctuating energy. It's an arena of violent activity that has a rich physical structure and can be described by physical laws. These particles are thought to originate by fluctuations of the energy in the vacuum."

So this wouldn't actually be an example of something coming into being out of nothing, with no cause. "The quantum vacuum and the energy locked up in the vacuum are the cause of these particles," Craig said. "And then we have to ask: What is the origin of the whole quantum vacuum itself? Where does *it* come from?"

Craig's answer made sense to me.

Step 2: The Universe Had a Beginning

Our conversation moved on to kalam's second statement. "Ever since the ancient Greeks," Craig said, "the assumption has been that the material world is eternal. Christians have denied this on the basis of biblical revelation. But secular science always assumed the universe's eternality. So the discovery in the twentieth century that the universe is *not* an unchanging, eternal entity was a complete shock to secular minds."

He added that there are essentially two pathways toward establishing the fact that the universe had a beginning. The first pathway could be called either mathematical or philosophical. The second pathway is the scientific.

He said early Christian and Muslim scholars used mathematical reasoning to demonstrate that it's impossible to have an infinite past. Therefore, the age of the universe had to be finite—the universe must have had a beginning.

Their reasoning came down to this: Since an infinite past would involve an infinite number of events, then the past simply can't be infinite. He gave me an illustration about marbles to help me understand this.

"Let's imagine I possessed an infinite number of marbles, and I wanted you to have an infinite number also. But if I gave you my entire (infinite) pile of marbles, I'd be left with zero marbles for myself."

In other words, in this case infinity minus infinity equals zero—a logical contradiction.

"But suppose we counted the marbles, then I gave you all the odd-numbered ones and kept all the evens. I would still have an infinity left over for myself, and you would have an infinity too—just as many as I have. In fact, each of us would have just as many as I had before we counted and divided them."

In this case, infinity minus infinity equals infinity—another logical contradiction.

"So then, suppose I gave you all the marbles except for

three that I like best. That way, you would have an infinity of marbles—but I end up with only three."

This time, infinity minus infinity equals three—yet another logical contradiction.

He summarized: "Substitute 'past events' for 'marbles,' and you can see the absurdities that would result. So the universe can't have an infinite number of events in its past. It must have had a beginning."

Craig added that the idea of an actual infinity exists only in our minds. Mathematicians can deal with infinite quantities in only an abstract way. "It's not descriptive of what can happen in the real world. And that's the point."

However, I spotted an inconsistency. "Then what about the idea of God being infinitely old? Doesn't your reasoning rule that out?"

"It rules out the concept of a God who has endured through an infinite past time," Craig answered. "But that's not the classic idea of God. Time and space are creations of God that began at the Big Bang. If you go back beyond the beginning of time itself, there's simply eternity—in the sense of timelessness. The eternal God is timeless in his being. God did not endure through an infinite amount of time up to the moment of creation; that would be absurd. God transcends time. He's beyond time. Once God creates the universe, he could enter time, but that's a different topic altogether."

Craig then turned to the pathway of science. We began discussing scientific evidence for the universe being created in the long-ago Big Bang. Craig mentioned a number of discoveries that have been pointing scientists toward this model since early in the twentieth century. He said predictions about the Big Bang have been consistently verified by scientific data, which alternative models have failed to disprove. "Unquestionably, the Big Bang model has impressive scientific credentials."

Step 3: Therefore, the Universe Has a Cause

We moved on to the third part of the kalam argument. Given that (1) whatever begins to exist has a cause, and that (2) the universe began to exist, then (3) there *must* be some sort of transcendent cause for the origin of the universe.

Craig even quoted an observation by an atheist, the philosopher Kai Nielsen: "Suppose you suddenly hear a loud bang, and you ask me, 'What made that bang?' and I reply, 'Nothing, it just happened.' You would not accept that."

"Nielsen's right, of course," Craig said. "And if a cause is needed for a small bang like that, then it's needed for the big one as well."

That conclusion seemed inescapable to me. And it confirms the Judeo-Christian doctrine—thousands of years old—of creation out of nothing.

Craig was looking at it logically: "A cause of space and time must be an uncaused, beginningless, timeless, spaceless, immaterial, personal being endowed with freedom of will and enormous power. And that is a core concept of God."

"Hold on!" I insisted. I brought up a point many atheists

make: If *everything* must have a cause, how does God get a free pass?

"They're missing the point!" Craig exclaimed. "The first premise of the kalam argument is *not* that *everything* has a cause—but that *whatever begins to exist* has a cause." He mentioned how atheists have long maintained that the universe doesn't need a cause because it's eternal. "So how can they possibly maintain that the *universe* can be eternal and uncaused—yet *God* cannot?"

Another objection popped into my mind. "Why does it have to be only one creator?"

Craig responded by mentioning a universally accepted scientific principle—that we shouldn't multiply causes beyond what's necessary to explain an observed effect. And with the universe, he said, "one creator is sufficient to explain the effect." He reminded me that the kalam argument doesn't say everything there is to say about the creator. "Nothing restricts us from looking at wider considerations."

My mind began raising more questions. I asked whether the kalam argument could tell us whether the creator is personal (as Christians believe), or he's just an impersonal force (as believed by many in the New Age movement).

This prompted Craig to point out the real difference between *scientific* explanations and *personal* explanations. "Scientific explanations explain a phenomenon in terms of certain initial conditions and natural laws that produced it. By contrast, personal explanations explain things by means of someone's volition or will."

He gave me an illustration. "Imagine walking into your mother's kitchen and you see a kettle boiling on the stove. You ask why the kettle's boiling, and she answers, 'Well, because the kinetic energy of the flame is conducted by the metal bottom of the kettle to the water, causing the water molecules to vibrate faster and faster until they're thrown off in the form of steam.' That would be a *scientific* explanation. Or she might say, 'I put it on to make a cup of tea.' That would be a personal explanation. Both are legitimate, but they explain the phenomenon in different ways."

Then Craig stated that there *cannot* be a scientific explanation of the beginning state of the universe. "Since it's the beginning state, it simply cannot be explained in terms of earlier initial conditions and natural laws leading up to it. So if there is an explanation of the first state of the universe, it *has* to be a personal explanation—that is, someone decided to create it."

He also gave me this line of reasoning: "The cause of the universe transcends time and space, so it cannot be a physical reality. Instead, it must be nonphysical or immaterial. And only two types of things can be timeless and immaterial: abstract objects like numbers, or a mind. But abstract objects can't cause anything to happen. So it makes sense that the universe is the product of an unembodied mind that brought it into existence."

He summarized it this way: "I can think of only one explanation for the origin of a finite universe from a timeless cause: That cause is a personal agent who has freedom of will. He can create a new effect without any predetermined conditions. He could decide to say, ‘Let there be light,’ and the universe would spring into existence.”

Craig added, “I’ve never seen a good response to this argument on the part of any atheist.”

CHAPTER 2

THE UNIVERSE NEEDS A FINE-TUNER

Bill Craig in Georgia had made a compelling case that the Big Bang points to the existence of God. Now I wanted to see evidence of whether the ongoing operation of our universe points in the same direction.

That search took me to see a gifted professor of physics in Oklahoma. We sat down to chat in the front room of his home.

Michael George Strauss, PhD, earned his doctorate in experimental high energy physics at UCLA. He then joined the faculty of the University of Oklahoma in 1995. He lectures around the world and has written an astonishing nine hundred scholarly articles on elementary particle physics.

He also performs research at the world's largest particle

physics laboratory, located near Geneva, Switzerland. There he smashes protons together in a particle collider (the world's largest) to better understand their properties.

Interestingly, Strauss's study of the world's tiniest particles has become more and more relevant to our understanding of the origin and order of the universe. This is because when the collider hurls protons together, the resulting energy density is so high that it is similar to what the universe was like a trillionth of a second after the Big Bang.

As we discussed how the universe operates, Strauss helped me understand just how fine-tuned it is: "Picture a control board with a hundred different dials and knobs, each one controlling a different aspect of physics. If you turn any of them just slightly to the left or right—*poof!* Intelligent life becomes impossible anywhere in the universe. Even just mistakenly bumping into one of those dials could make the world sterile and barren—or even nonexistent."

He continued, "Virtually every scientist agrees the universe is finely tuned. The question is, How did it get this way? The most plausible explanation is that the universe was designed by a creator."

I asked him for a few examples of this fine-tuning.

He brought up the amount of matter in the universe. "As the universe expands, all matter is attracted to other matter by gravity. If there were too much matter, the universe would collapse on itself before stars and planets could form. If there were too little matter, no star or planet could cohere. It turns out that shortly after the Big Bang, the amount of matter in the

"Virtually every scientist agrees the universe is finely tuned. The question is, How did it get this way? The most plausible explanation is that the universe was designed by a creator."

universe was precisely tuned to one part in a trillion trillion trillion trillion trillion. That's a ten with sixty zeros after it! In other words, throw in just a dime's worth of extra matter—and the universe wouldn't exist."

Nuclear Force at Work

Strauss also talked about the strong nuclear force, which is something he studies in his research. "This is what holds together the nucleus of atoms," he explained.

"What happens if you manipulate the strong nuclear force?" I asked.

"If you were to make it just two percent stronger, while all the other constants stayed the same, you'd add a lot more elements to the periodic table. But they would be radioactive and life-destroying. Plus, you'd have very little hydrogen in the universe—and without hydrogen, there's no water, no life."

"What if you turned the knob the other way?"

"Decrease the force by a mere five percent, and all you'd have would be hydrogen. Again, a dead universe."

Strauss's research also involves quarks, which make up neutrons and protons. "If we change the light quark mass just two or three percent," he said, "there would be no carbon in the universe." And no carbon would also mean no life.

The examples could go on and on.

Our Life-Sustaining Planet

Strauss told me that not only is our universe precisely calibrated to a breathtaking degree, but our planet is also amazingly situated so that life is possible.

"To have a planet like ours where life exists," he said, "first you need to be in the right kind of galaxy. There are three types of galaxies: elliptical, spiral, and irregular. You need to be in a spiral galaxy like we are because it's the only kind that produces the right heavy elements and has the right radiation levels.

"But you can't live just anywhere in the galaxy," he continued. "If you're too close to the center, there's too much radiation. And there's also a black hole, which you want to avoid. If you're too far from the center, you won't have the right so-called heavy elements. You'd lack the oxygen and carbon you'd need." What's required is a just-right "Goldilocks zone," or a "galactic habitable zone," where life can exist.

"Are you referring to intelligent life?" I asked.

"Anything more complex than bacteria," he said. "To have life, you need a star like our sun. Our sun is a class G star that has supported stable planet orbits in the right location for a long time. The star must be in its middle age, so its luminosity is stabilized. It has to be a bachelor star—many stars in the universe are binary, which means two stars orbiting each other, which is bad for stable planetary orbits. Plus, the star should be a third-generation star, like our sun."

"What does that mean?"

"The first generation of stars were made of hydrogen and helium from the Big Bang. They lasted only a relatively short time. The second generation created heavy elements like carbon, oxygen, silicon, iron, and other things we need. The third generation is made up of stars that have enough material to create rocky planets like Earth and carbon-based life-forms."

Strauss went on, "There are so many parameters that have to be just right for our planet to support life: the distance from the sun, the rotation rate, the amount of water, the tilt, the right size so gravity lets gases like methane escape but allows oxygen to stay."

He said there must also be a moon the size of ours to properly stabilize Earth's tilt. And amazingly, earthquakes and such are also needed; Strauss said this tectonic activity "drives biodiversity, helps avoid a water world without continents, and helps generate the magnetic field."

Another factor: "It's nice to have a huge planet like Jupiter nearby," Strauss said, "to act like a vacuum cleaner by attracting potentially devastating comets and meteors away from you."

Are There Other Planets Like Earth?

Like me, you may have heard news reports now and then about astronomers discovering an Earthlike planet somewhere in outer space. I brought this up to Strauss.

"Yes," he said, "but generally all they mean is that it has a similar size as Earth, or that it might be positioned to allow surface water. But there's so much more to Earth than those two factors."

By that he meant literally hundreds of conditions required for any planet to be truly like Earth. Strauss said that even if there were a billion trillion planets in the universe, "the odds of having any planet supporting higher life would be one in a million trillion."

He let that astonishing number sink in. "In science," he said, "we have a phrase for probabilities like that."

"Really? What is it?"

He grinned. "Ain't gonna happen."

The Multiverse Option

Although so many scientists recognize this amazing fine-tuning in our universe, they don't all see it as compelling evidence for the existence of God as creator. Some see another alternative: a "multiverse." They've proposed a theory that would allow for an almost infinite number of other universes. I brought this up to Strauss. If there really are that many universes, surely one of them sooner or later would get the right conditions for life.

Strauss responded that first of all, we don't know if the

multiverse model is correct. He said it was based on a controversial and incomplete concept called string theory, for which all the equations haven't been worked out. "There's no observational evidence for it," he said. "So is it really science?"

He continued, "Physicists have come up with various ideas for how multiverses could be birthed. But again, there's no observational or experimental evidence for it. In fact, there's likely no way for us to discover something that's beyond our universe.

"And even if there were multiple universes, they all must go back to one beginning point. So now we return to the question of who or what created the universe in the first place."

His conclusion: "If you want to believe in one of the multiverse theories, you basically need blind faith."

He added that even if the multiverse idea turns out to be true, it would actually support the case for a creator. "The extra dimensions of string theory would require that any creator exist in multiple dimensions. In fact, a discovery of other universes or extra dimensions would, in some sense, increase the necessary magnitude of any creator."

A Universe Too Big?

Meanwhile, Strauss is confident that if ours is the only universe—and, again, there's no scientific evidence that any others exist—then the fine-tuning of this universe is clear evidence that God is real. "Let's go back to what I know for a fact as a scientist," he said. "I know there's one universe that appears to have a beginning, which is incredibly calibrated in a way that defies naturalistic explanations. And there's a highly improbable planet whose unlikely conditions allow human life to exist. To me, all of that begs for a divine explanation."

I then raised a question. "Maybe our universe *isn't* so finely tuned. For instance, why would a creator waste so much space if he wanted to create a habitat for humankind? The universe is unimaginably huge, but it's largely a wasteland that's inhospitable to life."

"Actually," Strauss replied, "the universe is the smallest it could possibly be and still have life."

That statement shocked me, and I asked him to explain.

"If you start with the Big Bang," Strauss said, "and your goal is to make a solar system like ours, you have to go through two previous generations of stars. The first generation left behind some of the elements of the periodic table but lacked the right amounts of carbon, oxygen, and nitrogen to make rocky planets and complex life. Then the second generation of stars formed from the debris of the first generation. When these burned out, they made more heavy elements and scattered them throughout the universe. Our sun coalesced from that debris.

"Now here's my point," he continued. "This third generation of stars is the first possibility for a solar system like ours to exist. So if you start with the Big Bang, it takes 9 billion years for a solar system like ours to form. Scientists say that our solar system formed approximately 4.5 billion years ago. That adds up to about 13.5 billion years. So if you're God, and your purpose is to create Earth suitable for people, and you use these particular processes—that's how long it would take. And during that time, what is the universe doing?"

"Expanding," I answered.

"Right. It's getting bigger and bigger. So even though it's incredibly large, this is the youngest, and therefore the smallest, that the universe can be if you want to create one planet that's hospitable for life."

What Kind of God?

I then asked Strauss, "If God is the most likely explanation for our universe and planet, what can we logically deduce about him from the scientific evidence?"

"Several things," he said. "First, he must be transcendent, since he exists apart from his creation. Second, he must be immaterial or spirit, since he existed before the physical world. Third, he must be timeless or eternal, since he existed before physical time was created.

"Fourth, he must be powerful, given the immense energy of the Big Bang. Fifth, he must be smart, given the fact that the Big Bang was not some chaotic event but was finely tuned in a masterful way. Sixth, he must be personal, since a decision had to be made to create.

"Seventh, he must be creative. Just look at the wonders of the universe! And eighth, he must be caring, since he so purposefully crafted a habitat for us."

Plus, as Bill Craig said earlier, scientists agree that you shouldn't multiply causes beyond what's necessary to explain an effect—which means there would be just one creator.

All these qualities are consistent with the God of the Bible, the God of Christianity. Said Strauss: "If there's just one creator, that rules out polytheism [many gods]. Since he's outside of creation, this rules out pantheism [everything is god]. The universe is not cyclical, which violates the tenets of Eastern religions. And the Big Bang contradicts ancient religious assumptions that the universe is static."

All this rang true for me. Maybe it rings true for you as well, and perhaps you already see enough evidence for the fact that God is real.

But there's more to think about.

CHAPTER 3

OUR DNA DEMANDS A DESIGNER

Inside every one of our bodies are one hundred trillion cells. Inside each cell are six feet of tightly coiled microscopic DNA. As scientists have studied DNA, they marvel at how it provides the genetic information necessary to create all the proteins with which our bodies are built.

DNA serves as the information storehouse for a finely choreographed manufacturing process in which the right amino acids are linked together with the right bonds in the right sequence to produce the right kind of proteins that fold in the right way to build biological systems.

What evidence for God might there be in this kind of biological information found inside each cell of your body and mine? Where did that information come from? Was it mere evolution? Or some superintelligence?

The search for solid answers to these questions put me on a plane headed to the Pacific Northwest. In Seattle, I sat down with one of the country's foremost experts on origin-of-life issues.

Stephen C. Meyer, PhD, earned degrees in physics and geology, then went on to receive his master's degree in the history and philosophy of science at Cambridge University. He later obtained his doctorate from Cambridge, where he analyzed the scientific and methodological issues in origin-of-life biology.

Since then, he has become one of the most compelling voices in the intelligent design movement. His books include *Signature in the Cell*, which was named a Book of the Year by the *Times* [of London] *Literary Supplement*, and *The Return of the God Hypothesis.*

We began our discussion by acknowledging that finding the origin of life is about finding the source of biological information. Meyer compared it to how computer code works. "When I ask students what they would need to get their computer to perform a new function, they reply, 'You have to give it new lines of code.' The same principle is true in living organisms.

"If you want an organism to acquire a new function or structure, you have to provide information somewhere in the cell. You need instructions for how to build the cell's important components, which are mostly proteins.

"Ever since the 1950s and 1960s, biologists have recognized that the cell's critical functions are usually performed by proteins, and proteins are the product of assembly instructions stored in DNA. The digital code stored in DNA contains the instructions for telling the cell's machinery how to build proteins."

So DNA is necessary for life to begin. And Meyer believes that the source of information in DNA is best explained by an intelligent cause rather than by any naturalistic causes that scientists typically use to explain it.

I wanted to know more about this "information" in DNA. What did it look like?

Meyer said that DNA's information—the detailed instructions for assembling proteins—is stored in the form of a four-character digital code. He called this fact "one of the most extraordinary discoveries of the twentieth century."

He said these four characters "happen to be chemicals called adenine, guanine, cytosine, and thymine. Scientists represent them with the letters A, G, C, and T." They're arranged in a way to instruct the cell to build different sequences of amino acids, which are the building blocks of proteins. Different arrangements of these four characters will yield different sequences of amino acids.

"Essentially," he went on, "a protein is a long linear chain of amino acids. Because of the forces between the amino acids, the proteins 'fold' into very particular three-dimensional shapes. These three-dimensional shapes are highly irregular—sort of like the teeth in a key. And they have a lock-key fit with other molecules in the cell."

Different arrangements of the four characters in a different order would set up different kinds of interactions and folding.

"So the sequence of the amino acids," Meyer said, "is critical to getting the long chain to fold properly in order to form an actual functional protein. Wrong sequence, no folding—and the sequence of amino acids is unable to serve its function."

The Library of Life

I was fascinated by the process Meyer was describing. "DNA is like a library," he said. "The organism accesses the information it needs from DNA so it can build some of its critical components." To build a single protein, he said, what's typically needed is from 1,200 to 2,000 separate occurrences of the A, C, G, or T chemicals.

Our conversation turned again to the basic question of where that crucial information ultimately comes from. "It's *the* critical and foundational question," Meyer affirmed. "If you can't explain that, you haven't explained life, because the information is what makes the molecules into something that actually functions." He added that the information stored in DNA "or some other information carrier" is required in "even the very simplest cell we study today."

He confirmed his own belief that the presence of such information in a cell "is best explained by the activity of an intelligent agent."

But I wondered: Was there a chance scientists will someday find some better explanation—something better than intelligent design?

"DNA is like a library. The organism accesses the information it needs from DNA so it can build some of its critical components." And where does that crucial information ultimately come from? "It's *the* critical and foundational question. If you can't explain that, you haven't explained life."

"Yes, of course," Meyer said. But he added, "Origin-of-life scientists have looked at other possibilities for decades, and frankly, they've come up dry."

The Missing Soup

One possibility that some have proposed has to do with a so-called prebiotic soup. The idea is that basic organic compounds necessary for forming cells had accumulated in oceans on the ancient Earth. Over millions of years, basic life particles with ability to reproduce supposedly formed from this soup. These forms grew more complex until finally the first simple cell system emerged.

I asked Meyer about scientific evidence for this theory.

"There isn't any," he replied. For example, he said, "if this prebiotic soup had really existed, it would have been rich in amino acids. And therefore there would have been a lot of nitrogen, because amino acids are nitrogenous. So when we examine Earth's earliest sediments, we should find large deposits of nitrogen-rich minerals. Those deposits have never been located."

He added that "even if amino acids existed in the theoretical prebiotic soup, they would have readily reacted with other chemicals. This would have been another tremendous barrier to the formation of life."

Nevertheless, this idea of an ancient life-producing soup hangs on for many—which is "certainly surprising," Meyer said. He quoted from Michael Denton's book *Evolution: A Theory in Crisis* (p. 261): "Considering the way the prebiotic soup is referred to in so many discussions of the origin of life as an already established reality, it comes as something of a shock to realize that there is absolutely no positive evidence for its existence."

But what about other naturalistic explanations? Were there any more reasonable possibilities? Meyer discussed with me three proposed scenarios—random chance, natural selection, and the idea of self-ordering chemical affinities.

Random Chance

I mentioned the highly popular idea that life began simply by random chance. If you let amino acids randomly interact over millions of years, couldn't life somehow emerge?

Meyer said this theory has no scientific merit. "Virtually all origin-of-life experts have utterly rejected that approach." He said it was like trying to generate even a simple book by throwing Scrabble letters onto the floor. "Even a simple protein molecule, or the gene to build that molecule, is so rich in information that the entire time since the Big Bang would not give you the resources you would need to generate that molecule by chance."

But, I asked, if that first molecule had been far simpler than molecules today—wasn't it possible it could have formed randomly?

"Even a simple protein molecule, or the gene to build that molecule, is so rich in information that the entire time since the Big Bang would not give you the resources you would need to generate that molecule by chance."

In his answer, Meyer spoke of a "minimal complexity threshold" that would be necessary for a protein molecule to form by chance. He mentioned, for example, "a certain level of folding that a protein has to have, called tertiary structure, that is necessary for it to perform a function. You don't get tertiary structure in a protein unless you have at least seventy-five amino acids or so."

"For a protein molecule to form by chance," Meyer added, "you first need the right bonds between the amino acids. Second, amino acids come in right-handed and left-handed versions, and you've got to get only left-handed ones. Third, the amino acids must link up in a specified sequence, like letters in a sentence."

He gave me the odds of all these things falling into place on their own: "One chance in a hundred thousand trillion trillion trillion trillion trillion trillion trillion trillion trillion trillion. That's a ten with 125 zeros after it! And that would only be one protein molecule. A minimally complex cell would need between three hundred and five hundred protein molecules."

It would have to be some kind of "naturalistic miracle," he concluded.

Natural Selection

Although random chance by itself might not account for the origin of life—what about when it's combined with the process of natural selection? The famous biologist Richard Dawkins has suggested (in his book *Climbing Mount Improbable*) that in such a scenario, evolution is capable of accomplishing seemingly impossible tasks.

To that idea, Meyer responded this way: "Whether natural selection really works at the level of biological evolution is open to debate. But it most certainly does *not* work at the level of *chemical* evolution, which tries to explain the origin of the first life from simpler chemicals."

He pointed out that "natural selection requires a self-replicating organism to work. Organisms reproduce, and their offspring have variations. The ones that are better adapted to their environment survive better—and so those adaptations are preserved and passed on to the next generation. However, in order to have reproduction, there has to be cell division. And that presupposes the existence of information-rich DNA and proteins. But that's the problem—those are the very things they're trying to explain!

"You've got to have a self-replicating organism for Darwinian evolution to take place, but you can't have a self-replicating organism until you have the information necessary in DNA, which is what you're trying to explain in the first place."

He pictured it this way: "It's like the guy who falls into a deep hole and realizes he needs a ladder to get out. So he climbs out, goes home, gets a ladder, jumps back into the hole, and climbs out. It begs the question."

Chemical Affinities and Self-Ordering

Meyer pointed out that by the early 1970s, most origin-of-life scientists had become disenchanted with the options of random chance and natural selection. So some of them explored a third possibility. They offered theories that chemical attractions might have caused DNA's four-letter alphabet to self-assemble, or that the natural affinities between amino acids caused them to link together by themselves to create protein.

Meyer said there are examples in nature where chemical attractions do result in a kind of self-ordering. Salt crystals are a good illustration. Chemical forces of attraction cause sodium ions (Na^+) to bond with chloride ions (Cl^-) in order to form highly ordered patterns within a crystal of salt. You get a sequence of Na and Cl repeating over and over.

But he said that when scientists did experiments, they found that amino acids didn't demonstrate these same bonding affinities. There were very slight affinities, but they didn't match any of the known sequencing patterns found in functional proteins.

Besides, some scientists raised the question that even if this kind of self-organization could explain the sequencing in DNA and proteins—wouldn't we end up with something like a crystal of salt continually repeating?

"If all you had were repeating characters in DNA," Meyer explained, "the assembly instructions would merely tell amino acids to link in the same way over and over. You wouldn't be able to build all the many different kinds of protein molecules you need for a living cell to function."

He summarized: "Self-organization gives you repetitive, redundant structure, which is known as simple order. But information requires variability, irregularity, and unpredictability—that is, *complexity.* And complexity and simple order are opposites."

Our discussion had revealed that no explanation so far comes close to explaining how information necessary for life's origin arose by naturalistic means. "But maybe someday," I said to Meyer, "scientists will come up with another hypothesis."

"Maybe they will," he replied. "Though we do know that some possibilities can be excluded. They're dead ends."

I pointed out an objection. "Some skeptics would claim that you're arguing from ignorance. Scientists don't know for sure how life started, so you conclude there must have been an intelligent designer."

But Meyer insisted he wasn't arguing from ignorance. "I'm not saying intelligent design makes sense simply because other theories fail." Instead, he said he was pointing to the best available explanation— "which is how scientists reason in historical matters. Based on the evidence, the scientist assesses each hypothesis on the basis of its ability to explain the evidence at hand."

We had explored how neither chance, nor chance combined with natural selection, nor self-organizational processes could cause information to be produced. "But," Meyer said, "we do know of one entity that does have the required causal powers to produce information—and that's *intelligence*. We're arriving at this explanation *not* on the basis of what we don't know, but on the basis of what we know. That's not an argument from ignorance."

ability to produce information—and that's intelligence. We are arriving at this explanation not on the basis of what we don't know, but on the basis of what we know. It's not an argument from ignorance."

CHAPTER 4

EASTER SHOWED THAT JESUS IS GOD

Stephen Meyer had made a convincing case that intelligence—and intelligence alone—could explain the presence of precise information within genetic material. Taken together with what I'd learned about the origin of the universe and about its fine-tuning, the case for God being real seemed all the more powerful and persuasive.

Although these scientific findings make theism (belief in one God as creator) the best possible explanation for our world, they fall short of establishing the overall credibility of Christianity. For that, I knew I needed to turn to history to investigate the core claim of the Christian faith—that Jesus of Nazareth proved his divinity by rising from the dead. If Jesus claimed to be God before he died, and then rose from the dead—well, that's convincing evidence that he was telling the truth.

To help analyze the historical data, I met with one of the leading scholars on the resurrection. Michael R. Licona, PhD, earned his doctorate on the resurrection from the University of Pretoria in South Africa. Licona was mentored by Gary Habermas, one of the world's leading resurrection authorities. Together, they wrote the award-winning book *The Case for the Resurrection of Jesus*. Licona himself later wrote *The Resurrection of Jesus: A New Historiographical Approach*, a landmark work on the topic.

In recent years, Licona has debated Shabir Ally (a fierce defender of Islam), atheist activist Dan Barker, historian Richard Carrier (who believes that Jesus never existed), and agnostic scholar Bart Ehrman.

Licona's own faith was sharpened by a period of doubt he went through decades ago, following his graduate studies. His questions about the truth of Christianity nearly prompted him to abandon the beliefs he'd held since childhood. His renewed investigation into Christianity and other major world religions, as well as his in-depth study of atheism, ended up solidifying his conviction that Christianity rests on a firm historical foundation.

Some Basics for Doing History

As our conversation began, Licona discussed some basics for doing good history. He explained a "minimal facts approach" to help historians overcome any bias they may have about what they're researching.

"Under this approach," Licona said, "we consider only the facts that meet two criteria. First, there must be very strong historical evidence supporting them. And second, this evidence must be accepted as historical facts by the vast majority of today's scholars on the subject—including skeptical ones."

He said the next step is to try coming up with the best historical explanation to account for these facts. "It's like putting together a jigsaw puzzle. Each piece represents a historical fact, and we want to put them together in a way that doesn't leave out any pieces and doesn't require us to force any of the pieces to make them fit. In the end, the puzzle creates a picture that's based on the best explanation for the facts we have."

I asked Licona how strong a case he could build—using only "minimal facts"—for Jesus rising from the dead.

He replied, "I'll use just five minimal facts—and you can decide for yourself how persuasive the case is."

1. Jesus's Crucifixion and Death

Licona mentioned various authors today who are atheists or skeptics or agnostics, and yet who hold Jesus's crucifixion to be historical fact. He said they support this first of all because the crucifixion is reported by all four of the Gospels in the New Testament. The Gospels are viewed broadly by historians as "a set of ancient documents that can be subjected to historical scrutiny like any other accounts from antiquity."

He also spoke of ancient non-Christian sources that mention the killing of Jesus. These include the Roman historian Tacitus, the Jewish historian Josephus, and two writers (Lucian of Samosata and Mara Bar-Serapion) in the Roman province of Syria. The ancient Jewish theology text known as the Talmud reports that "Yeshu was hanged." (*Yeshu* is a Hebrew equivalent to *Jesus*, and the phrase "hung on a tree" often referred to crucifixion, as it does in Galatians 3:13 in our New Testament.)

"The scholarly consensus is absolutely overwhelming," Licona said. "This first fact is as solid as anything in ancient history: Jesus was crucified and died as a result."

2. Belief by Jesus's Disciples That He Rose and Appeared to Them

"The second fact," Licona said, "is the disciples' belief that Jesus had actually returned from the dead and had appeared to them." He pointed to three strands of evidence for this: (1) Paul's testimony about the disciples; (2) oral traditions that passed through the early church; and (3) the written works of the early church.

He said Paul's testimony is important "because he reports knowing some of the disciples personally, including Peter,

"The scholarly consensus is absolutely overwhelming. This first fact is as solid as anything in ancient history: Jesus was crucified and died as a result."

James, and John, as we see in Acts 9:26–30 and 15:1–35. And in writing to the Corinthians about Christ's resurrection, Paul joined himself with other apostles in declaring, "This is what we preach" (1 Corinthians 15:11). In other words, Paul *knew* those apostles and could testify to their shared claim—that Jesus had returned from the dead."

As for oral (spoken) tradition, Licona noted how much people in those days relied on verbal transmission for passing along what was important to remember. "Scholars have identified several places in which this oral tradition has been copied into the New Testament in the form of creeds, hymns, and sermon summaries. This is really significant, because the oral tradition must therefore have existed prior to the New Testament writings."

As an example, he referred again to 1 Corinthians 15, where we find "one of the earliest and most important creeds" of the church. This would have been reported to the Corinthian church by Paul in about AD 55, when he said:

> For what I received I passed on to you as of first importance: that Christ died for our sins according to the Scriptures, that he was buried, that he was raised on the third day according to the Scriptures, and that he appeared to Cephas [Peter], and then to the Twelve. After that, he appeared to more than five hundred of the brothers and sisters at the same time, most of whom are still living, though some have fallen asleep. Then he appeared to James, then to all the apostles. (1 Corinthians 15:3–7)

"Many scholars believe Paul received this creed from Peter and James while visiting with them in Jerusalem three years after his conversion [a visit mentioned in Galatians 1:18]. That would be within five years of the crucifixion." Licona added, "Not only is this creed extremely early, but it was apparently given to Paul by eyewitnesses or others he deemed reliable, which heightens its credibility even more." Licona said this creed "can practically be traced to the original disciples of Jesus. In fact, this creed has been one of the most formidable obstacles to critics who try to shoot down the resurrection. It's simply gold for a historian."

The New Testament also preserves several sermons of the apostles. "The vast majority of historians believe that the apostles' early teachings are enshrined in these sermon summaries in Acts—which clearly declare that Jesus rose bodily from the dead." (For example, compare the words preached by Peter in Acts 2:22–32 with words preached by Paul in Acts 13:34–38.)

Besides these oral traditions, we also have of course the written sources of Matthew, Mark, Luke, and John. "It's widely accepted," Licona said, "even among skeptical historians, that these Gospels were written in the first century. So we have biographies written within seventy years of Jesus's life that unambiguously report the disciples' claims that Jesus rose from the dead."

(By comparison, Licona said our two best sources on Alexander the Great weren't written until at least four hundred years after his life. For Rome's Caesar Augustus, historians' chief sources are a document written between fifty and a hundred years after his death, and three others written between a hundred and two hundred years after he died.)

Licona also mentioned the writings of "the apostolic fathers"—church leaders who personally knew the apostles or were close to others who did. "There's a strong likelihood that their writings reflect the teachings of the apostles themselves. And what do they say? That the apostles were dramatically impacted by Jesus's resurrection."

One example was a man named Polycarp, who lived in the late first and early second centuries. Much was written about Polycarp by the second-century Christian leader Irenaeus (who was a young man when he first heard Polycarp preach). Irenaeus said that Polycarp was "instructed by the apostles, and conversed with many who had seen Christ"—including the apostle John. Polycarp "recalled their very words," Irenaeus reported, and "always taught the things which he had learned from the apostles."

In a letter written by Polycarp around AD 110, he mentions Christ's resurrection several times. And concerning Paul and the apostles he writes that "they did not love the present age, but him who died for our benefit and for our sake was raised by God."

Licona noted how Christ's resurrection "is something the disciples believed to the core of their being. We have evidence that the disciples had been transformed to the point where they were willing to endure persecution and even martyrdom.

We find this in multiple accounts inside and outside the New Testament."

We see in the book of Acts, for example, "how the disciples were willing to suffer for their conviction that Jesus rose from the dead. The church fathers Clement, Polycarp, Ignatius, Tertullian, and Origen—they all confirm this. In fact, we've got at least seven early sources testifying that the disciples willingly suffered in defense of their beliefs. And if we include the martyrdoms of Paul and Jesus's half brother James, we have eleven sources."

But I raised an objection with Licona. "People of other faiths have also been willing to die for their beliefs through the ages. So what does the suffering of the disciples really prove?"

He responded, "First, it means that they certainly regarded their beliefs to be true. They didn't willfully lie about this. Liars make poor martyrs. Second, the disciples didn't just *believe* Jesus rose from the dead; they knew this for a fact. They were on the scene and able to ascertain for sure that he had been resurrected. So it was for the *truth* of the resurrection that they were willing to die."

He contrasted this with modern-day Islamic terrorists or others willing to die for their beliefs. "These people have faith that their beliefs are true, but they aren't in a position to know that for sure. The disciples of Jesus, on the other hand, knew for a *fact* that Christ's resurrection had truly occurred. And knowing the *truth*, they were willing to die for it."

"The disciples were willing to suffer for their conviction that Jesus rose from the dead. The church fathers Clement, Polycarp, Ignatius, Tertullian, and Origen—they all confirm this. In fact, we've got at least seven early sources testifying that the disciples willingly suffered in defense of their beliefs."

3. The Conversion of the Church Persecutor Paul

The third minimal fact: "We know from multiple sources," Licona said, "that Paul—then known as Saul of Tarsus—was an enemy of the church and committed to persecuting the faithful. But Paul himself said that he was converted to a follower of Jesus because he personally encountered the resurrected Jesus. [You can explore this in chapters 9, 22, and 26 in Acts, plus 1 Corinthians 9:1 and 15:8.] So we have Jesus's resurrection attested by friend and foe alike, which is very significant."

In addition to Paul, Licona mentioned other ancient sources (including Luke and Polycarp) reporting that Paul was willing to suffer continuously and even die for his beliefs. "Again, liars make poor martyrs. We can be confident not only that Paul claimed the risen Jesus appeared to him, but that he really believed it."

I pointed out that people convert to other religions all the time. "What's so special about Paul?"

What's special here, Licona said, is that "Paul was transformed by a personal encounter with the risen Christ. His conversion is based in *primary* evidence—Jesus directly appeared to him. That's a big difference."

Paul's mindset was to oppose the Christian movement, because he believed they were following a false messiah. "His radical transformation from persecutor to missionary demands an explanation," Licona said. "And I think the best explanation is that he told the truth when he said he met the risen Jesus on the road to Damascus. He had nothing to gain in this world—except his own suffering and martyrdom—from making this up."

4. The Conversion of the Skeptic James, Jesus's Half Brother

Licona's fourth minimal fact involves James, the half brother of Jesus. "We have good evidence," Licona said, "that James was not a follower of Jesus during Jesus's lifetime. Mark and John both report that none of Jesus's brothers believed in him." (We see this in Mark 3:21, 3:31, and 6:3–4, and in John 7:3–5.)

These reports can be considered authentic, Licona said, "because of the principle of embarrassment. People aren't likely to invent a story that will be embarrassing or potentially discrediting to them. And it would be particularly humiliating for a first-century rabbi not to have his own family as his followers."

In the ancient creedal material we looked at from 1 Corinthians 15, we're told that the risen Jesus appeared to James. Again, this is an extremely early account that has all the earmarks of reliability.

"As a result of his encounter, James doesn't just become a Christian, but he later becomes leader of the Jerusalem church." (We know this from Acts 15:12–21 and Galatians 1:19.) "James was so thoroughly convinced of Jesus's messiahship because of the resurrection that he died as a martyr, as both Christian and non-Christian sources attest."

5. The Empty Tomb of Jesus

Licona advanced to the last of his minimal facts. Licona acknowledged that this fifth fact—that the tomb of Jesus was empty—doesn't enjoy the almost universal consensus among scholars that the first four do. "Still," Licona said, "there's strong evidence in its favor."

He said that his mentor Gary Habermas has determined that about 75 percent of scholars on the subject regard the empty tomb as a historical fact. "That's quite a large majority. Personally, I think the empty tomb is very well supported if the historical data is assessed without preconceptions." He cited three strands of evidence.

"First is the fact that Jesus was publicly executed and buried in Jerusalem, with his resurrection proclaimed afterward in the very same city. In fact, several weeks after the crucifixion, Peter declares to a crowd right there in Jerusalem, 'God has raised this Jesus to life, and we are all witnesses of it' [Acts 2:32]. Frankly, it would have been impossible for Christianity to get off the ground in Jerusalem if Jesus's body were still in the tomb. The Roman or Jewish authorities could have simply gone to his tomb and viewed his corpse, and the misunderstanding would have been over. But there's no indication that this occurred."

Instead, Licona stated, what we hear is enemies of Jesus *attesting* to the empty tomb. They were saying that the disciples stole the body, something reported not only in the Gospel of Matthew but also by the church fathers Justin Martyr and

Tertullian. "Why would you say someone stole the body if it were still in the tomb? This is an implicit admission that the tomb was empty."

Besides, Licona added, the stolen body explanation is a lame one. "Are we supposed to believe they stole the body and then they were willing to suffer continuously and even die for what they knew was a lie? That's such an absurd idea that scholars universally reject it today."

A third strand of evidence is the testimony from women that the tomb was empty. "Not only were women the first to discover the vacant grave," said Licona, "but they are mentioned in all four of the Gospels, whereas male witnesses appear only later, and in only two of the Gospels."

This is important, Licona added, "because in both first-century Jewish and Roman cultures, women were lowly esteemed, and their testimony was considered very questionable. They were certainly considered less credible than men. So if you were going to concoct a story in an effort to fool others, back then you would never have hurt your credibility by saying that women discovered the empty tomb. If the writers of the Gospels had felt free simply to make things up, surely they'd claim that men—maybe Peter or John—were the first to find the tomb empty." Here was another example of the principle of embarrassment.

Now that we had looked at these minimal facts, Licona said that we needed to ask ourselves this question: What's the best explanation for the evidence—the explanation that doesn't leave out any of the facts or strains to make anything fit?

"My conclusion," he said, "based on the evidence, is that Jesus did return from the dead. No other explanation comes close to accounting for all the facts. Historically speaking, I think we've got a convincing case."

More Objections

A common challenge to this conclusion is the idea that the disciples didn't really encounter the resurrected Jesus; they were merely hallucinating. I asked Licona if this could account for the appearances of Jesus.

In reply, he said that hallucinations can't be shared by multiple people, and yet scholars have at least three instances when the risen Jesus appeared to groups.

"Hallucinations are not contagious," Licona continued. "They're personal. They're like dreams. On top of that, hallucinations can't account for the empty tomb. They can't account for the appearance to Paul, because he wasn't grieving—he was occupied with trying to destroy the church. And in the midst of that, he believes he sees the risen Jesus. James was a skeptic. He wasn't in the frame of mind for hallucinations."

I moved on to another popular objection. "Why," I asked Licona, "should the story of Jesus's resurrection have any more credibility than pagan stories of dying and rising gods—such as Osiris, Adonis, Attis, and Marduk?" Those ancient stories are so obviously mythological—and some critics say

Christianity is merely a copycat religion that took the resurrection idea from them.

Licona was well versed on this controversy. "First of all, it's important to understand that these claims don't in any way negate the good historical evidence we have for Jesus's resurrection that I've spelled out."

He mentioned also a book called *The Riddle of Resurrection* by Swedish scholar Tryggve N. D. Mettinger. It's one of the most recent academic treatments of dying and rising gods in antiquity. Mettinger acknowledges in his book that the consensus among modern scholars—nearly universal—is that there were no dying and rising gods that preceded Christianity. They all came after the first century.

Obviously, that timing is crucial.

However, Licona said, "Mettinger then takes a minority position and claims that there are at least three and possibly as many as five dying and rising gods that *do* predate Christianity. But the key question is this: Are there any actual parallels between these myths and Jesus's resurrection? After combing through all these accounts and critically analyzing them, Mettinger states that none of these serve as parallels to Jesus. *None* of them. They are far different from the reports of Jesus rising from the dead."

For example, Licona said they occurred in the unspecified and distant past and were usually related to the seasonal life-and-death cycle of vegetation. "In contrast, Jesus's resurrection wasn't repeated, wasn't related to changes in the seasons, and was sincerely believed to be an actual event by those who lived in the same generation of the historical Jesus."

In addition, Mettinger had stated, "There is no evidence for the death of the dying and rising gods as vicarious suffering for sins."

I later obtained Mettinger's book to double-check Licona's account. Sure enough, Mettinger caps his study by stating that there is no apparent evidence "as far as I am aware . . . that the death and resurrection of Jesus is a mythological construct, drawing on the myths and rites of the dying and rising gods of the surrounding world." Mettinger ultimately affirmed that "the faith in the death and resurrection of Jesus retains its unique character in the history of religions."

His analysis is a sharp rebuke of popular-level authors and internet bloggers who make grand claims about the pagan origins of Jesus's return from the dead.

For me, the verdict in the case for the resurrection is that Jesus did, indeed, return from the dead. He vindicated his own claim to be divine.

It seemed clear: Yes, God is real—and Jesus is his unique Son.

CHAPTER 5

EXPERIENCING GOD

For some people, their own profound spiritual experience has dramatically opened their eyes to the fact that God is real. For many, the proof that God exists is their experience with God after their conversion. They find a profound sense of community with him as he brings transformation into their lives.

Many theologians believe that the best explanation for these various religious experiences is that they reflect a genuine encounter with divine reality. Skeptics, however, tend to write off these phenomena as being unreliable or having some sort of naturalistic explanation.

What about you? Are you open to the possibility that religious experiences can provide meaningful evidence that God is real? Have you had an experience like this yourself?

Philosopher Douglas Groothuis, PhD, is among the scholars who believe that certain religious experiences can offer clear evidence for God's existence. To explore this further with Groothuis, I flew to Colorado, where he was then teaching at Denver Seminary.

My first interview with him (for a different book) had been under difficult circumstances. His wife, Rebecca, was dying of a brain condition, and Groothuis spoke to me in a candid way about their emotional anguish. His wife ended up dying shortly after our time together.

Now, years later, Groothuis was more animated and upbeat. He has remarried, and he seems as fully engaged with his work as ever. He has authored twenty books. My favorite is his hefty *Christian Apologetics: A Comprehensive Case for Biblical Faith*.

We talked first about what makes experiences with God possible—and even natural.

Groothuis brought up a basic point made by twentieth-century theologian and philosopher Francis Schaeffer: *God is infinite and personal, and we are finite and personal.* "Because of that," Groothuis said, "we have the potential of connecting on a personal, relational level. Being made in God's image opens the door to communion with him—despite the fractures in our relationship caused by our sin."

He said this gives us the possibility of gaining knowledge about God not only through the Bible and through what we see in nature, but also "through having personal experiences with the God who conceived us and created us."

He added, "We see contemporary accounts of amazing experiences with God all around the world. For example, there are Jesus dreams occurring among Muslims in closed cultures—this is a well-documented phenomenon.

"We see God breaking into the lives of people in a dramatic manner. And we also see more subtle experiences of God. Christians talk all the time about how God encourages, convicts, or guides them, or he gives them courage or peace, or he otherwise manifests himself in their lives. In fact, Christians undergo what's called a 'transformational experience.'"

Groothuis said that such personal transformation goes along with Christian belief, repentance, and religious commitment. "The Bible promises an abundant life in Christ [as we see in John 10:10], and Christians experience significant changes in their lives and attribute these changes to the influence of God. They typically report a new moral awareness and progress, a sense of guidance or calling, and a deep sense of belonging to God. The Bible says [in Galatians 5:22–23] that over time Christians will experience increased love, joy, peace, patience, kindness, goodness, faithfulness, gentleness, and self-control. This is to be expected if the Christian message is true."

Peace That Passes Understanding

I then asked Groothuis, "Have you had personal experiences of God?"

He answered, "I've been a Christian since 1976, and I've been through my share of difficulties and challenges. Through it all, though, I've heard God speak to me through Scripture,

"We see contemporary accounts of amazing experiences with God all around the world. We see God breaking into the lives of people in a dramatic manner. And we also see more subtle experiences of God."

through sermons, and through the wisdom of godly friends. And at times the experience is more profound."

"Can you give me an example?"

"I remember a prayer meeting around 1990 when several of us were fasting and praying for a friend who was quite ill. I remember going home and waking up the next day and thinking, *Something's strange.* I've struggled with anxiety for much of my life, and at the time I was in a very stressful period as I worked on my doctorate. And yet starting that day and continuing for two weeks, I felt absolutely no worry or anxiety. There was such an incredible sense of freedom and joy in the Lord like I'd never known before. After two weeks, it was gone, but I attribute that experience to a special presence of the Holy Spirit in that prayer meeting."

Groothuis said that such occasional visitations of the Holy Spirit "can be quite moving, though I would caution that Christians shouldn't try to live off them. If they do, they might start pursuing spiritual highs, and encounter counterfeits or stray outside of biblical doctrine."

I asked if he had specifically experienced moments of peace and strength in various ways during the time when his wife's health was deteriorating.

"I did," he replied, "but not regularly and not in exceptional ways. For us, it was the hope that God infused into our lives—a *rational* hope. The hope of the gospel, the hope of a resurrected body, the hope of a new heaven and a new earth. Hope was the experience for us, more than joy or even peace. And that hope sustained us in remarkable ways."

Testing Our Experiences

Groothuis spoke more about the need for such experiences with God to be authentic—so that "it conveys truth and is not deceptive, like a mirage of a pool of water that a thirsty person imagines in the desert." He mentioned the teaching in 1 John 4:1. "The Bible says we're supposed to test the spirits to determine whether they're really from God."

I asked how we can evaluate experiences with God to know whether they're trustworthy.

Groothuis answered by outlining four ways to categorize claims of religious experiences. "First, someone may be lying. Second, a person may have an experience that's purely subjective, like a hallucination or mirage, and incorrectly think it's an encounter with God. Third, someone may experience something extraordinary but not divine, and yet incorrectly attribute it to God. And fourth, a person may experience an actual divine reality."

That fourth category, he said, is what philosophers consider "numinous" experiences. "It means experiencing a transfixing or even frightening object that is distinct from the person experiencing it. In other words, there's the subject who has the experience; there's the conscious experience of the numinous; and then there's the numinous object itself."

He added, "The key is that these are encounters with something that's objectively outside the person. It's not just conjured up by someone's overactive imagination. A numinous experience can be a conduit for knowledge because there's a relationship between a subject and an object."

As an example of this, he spoke of the experience of the prophet Isaiah as described in Isaiah 6. "He sees the Lord exalted, seated on a throne, and angels calling out 'Holy, holy, holy is the LORD Almighty; the whole earth is full of his glory.' Isaiah falls on his face and declares, 'Woe to me! I am ruined! . . . My eyes have seen the King, the LORD Almighty.'" Groothuis pointed out that in this situation "there's Isaiah, who's distinct from God; there's his conscious experience of meeting God; and then there's God, who is objectively real and separate from Isaiah."

I pondered for a moment this concept of the numinous experience. "Would this mean that religious experiences of Hindus and Buddhists wouldn't qualify?"

"That's right," said Groothuis. "In Eastern mysticism, the whole notion of self disappears, as does the knowable object. The subject-object relationship is swallowed up by the void. Mystics talk about pure consciousness and experiences that cannot be described. That's a million miles away from the kind of experience Isaiah had."

The important distinction about Christian experiences, Groothuis stressed, is that "they involve an encounter with an external and personal being of transcendent significance."

I asked, "Should we be skeptical about a religious experience if we have one?"

"We can take that caution too far," he replied. He

mentioned the "principle of credulity" proposed by British philosopher Richard Swinburne in his book *The Existence of God*. Groothuis expressed the principle this way: "Unless there's good evidence to the contrary, if a person seems to experience something, they should believe it's probably authentic. So we should generally take our experiences to be truth-conveying unless there is a reason to think otherwise. In the case of a religious experience, if I believe I've encountered God in one way or the other, then all things being equal, I should suppose that I probably did encounter God."

"But," I said, "you might be mistaken."

"Sure. But we can't consider all truth claims and experiences to be false until proven true. We don't typically go through life treating every experience that way. It's unworkable." Groothuis mentioned the "principle of testimony"—also from Swinburne—"which says that all things being equal, we don't assume people are lying or are deceived. If someone says they experienced God in a particular way, we shouldn't assume they're deceived or lying unless we have indications that there's falsehood involved."

He said one test of whether an experience with God is authentic is to weigh it against the teachings of Scripture, since we have solid reasons for trusting the Bible's reliability. "The Bible becomes *the* guide for testing the validity of an experience," he said. "Whatever experience occurs, if it's really from God, it will not contradict the Bible."

Groothuis added this caution: "Whenever we weigh the legitimacy of an experience, we need to do it against the

"We should generally take our experiences to be truth-conveying unless there is a reason to think otherwise. In the case of a religious experience, if I believe I've encountered God in one way or the other, then all things being equal, I should suppose that I probably did encounter God."

background evidence for the existence of God. If the evidence were to point away from God being real, then obviously this would be a good reason to discount the authenticity of any religious experience. We have multiple reasons for believing in God's existence."

He said we therefore shouldn't be surprised if we actually encounter him. "So many people of all backgrounds have reported experiences of God around the world and throughout history."

This brought to mind various cases I've researched through the years, such as the Muslim woman in Egypt who encountered Jesus in a supernatural dream. When she asked him to tell her more, he pointed to a man beside him and said, "Ask my friend tomorrow about me."

The next day in the crowded Cairo marketplace, the woman saw the man from her dream, with the same clothes and glasses. She said to him, "You're the one! You were in my dream last night!" It so happened he was a Christian missionary who instantly realized she had had a dream about Jesus. In fact, the only reason he was visiting the marketplace that day was because he felt God had a special assignment for him. In the end, he was able to share the gospel with the Muslim woman for three hours.

This is typical of the "Jesus dreams" happening in Islamic countries. People don't go to sleep as a Muslim and awaken as a Christian; rather, their dream points them toward somebody who subsequently teaches them from the Bible. This validates their personal experience in the dream.

A Scientific Test?

We also discussed the fact that because religious experiences typically happen at an unpredictable time to one individual, this means they aren't repeatable, they can't be measured, and they can't be scientifically tested.

"After all," Groothuis said, "God is an invisible personal being who chooses when and where he wants to reveal himself. We can't put him under a microscope or in a test tube."

But Groothuis mentioned a further step to test religious experiences: "We can compare the experience to the long tradition of religious experiences within Christianity, going all the way back to the Bible. Is the experience at least consistent with this basic tradition, even though there might be differences? We can also investigate to see if there are any surrounding factors that would challenge the credibility of an experience."

"Such as—what?"

"Was the person under the influence of drugs? Does he or she have a history of deceiving people or having mental illness? Are peripheral details—like when and where the person had the experience—shown to be inaccurate? Does the individual have something to gain from sharing the experience? Obviously, these things would cast doubt on their report."

Groothuis added, "We also have to keep in mind that religious experiences are only one avenue of evidence for a religious worldview. We have to pursue other lines of argumentation and evidence."

He gave this example: "Let's say a Mormon missionary encourages you to read the Book of Mormon and see whether you experience a 'burning in the bosom' that supposedly confirms its authenticity. Even if you felt a warming in your heart, that experience wouldn't be confirmation that Mormon teachings are true. It wouldn't overcome the lack of historical and archaeological support for the Book of Mormon. So religious experience needs to be weighed against other relevant sources of evidence."

I asked him also about evaluating the validity of Eastern mystical experiences.

He answered, "The enlightenment experiences of both *nirvana* in Buddhism and *moksha* in Hinduism require the negation of individuality, personality, and language. There's no personal encounter with another being of immense holiness and power. If a mystical experience is devoid of any intellectual content, it can't possibly serve as logical evidence for any worldview."

He compared this with Christianity: "If you ask why I believe Christianity is true, religious experiences are not the first evidence I'd mention. Initially, I'd talk about the kind of evidence that Christian philosophers typically offer—evidence about the origin and fine-tuning of the universe, the existence of objective morality, the resurrection, and so forth."

He added that religious experiences by themselves don't offer conclusive proof. "They're *part* of the case, but they're not *the* case. Still, they're one more persuasive category of evidence which affirms that Christianity is true."

The Psychology of Religious Experiences

Throughout history there have been influential people who tried to undermine the legitimacy of religious experiences. They view such experiences as simply a projection of our psychological needs and desires. For example, the psychoanalyst Sigmund Freud believed that religious beliefs are an illusion, and he noted a century ago (in his book *The Future of an Illusion*) that "what is characteristic of illusions is that they are derived from human wishes."

But Groothuis said that such an explanation "falls flat for a number of reasons." He noted that people such as Freud and Karl Marx "thought religious belief was based on superstition. They thought that because there's no evidential weight behind it, they could explain away faith as being purely psychological. But we know that's not true. I've written an 846-page book on the historical, philosophical, and scientific reasons that support Christianity."

He noted also that "just because we have a strong wish for X doesn't mean that X can't be true. It's possible for a person to come to God because of a deep psychological need, such as a quest for love or acceptance, and still hold a true belief."

He raised another point: "There are aspects of Christianity that are not good candidates for wish fulfillment. If I were creating a religion, there are a lot of features of Christianity I'd leave out. Like how strict Jesus is about our thoughts and our anger—he says that vicious thoughts are equivalent to vicious acts [as we see in Matthew 5:22]. And I certainly wouldn't invent a religion where some of my friends might end up in hell. But the Bible often goes against the grain of what we want. And numinous experiences are often a shock to the person experiencing them. You can't tame God."

Besides, he added, "the charge of psychological projection against Christians can be turned against the skeptic. Given the fact that the vast majority of humanity has believed in God and the supernatural, it seems more likely that it's the atheists who suffer from some psychological disorder that makes belief in God difficult for them."

CHAPTER 6

WHICH GOD IS REAL?

With so many different religious beliefs in the world, why should people trust Christianity?

In other words, *which* God is real?

That's the question that led me to Indiana to visit Christian philosopher and world religions expert Chad V. Meister, PhD. With his incisive mind, gentle humor, and warm personality, Meister is among the most popular teachers at Bethel University, where he serves as professor of theology and philosophy. He's the author, coauthor, or editor of more than twenty books.

The first book he wrote was *Building Belief: Constructing Faith from the Ground Up*. That title matches what God has done in Meister's own journey of faith.

He grew up questioning the reality of God. As a young man he battled depression and was on the verge of suicide. With gun in hand, he cried out in anguish to God—and received a vision directing him to a certain verse in the Bible (a book he'd never read and didn't own). The verse was Acts 14:22—"We must go through many hardships to enter the kingdom of God." After putting down the gun, then going to find a Bible, he located and read the verse. It made him realize that God was pursuing him. His depression lifted, and he committed his life to God. In time he married a Christian woman, and together they attended church.

His young faith, however, was severely tested by conversations and encounters with people from other religions, especially his well-educated Hindu boss. This boss powerfully expressed the beauty and wonder of the Hindu religion, which left Meister's head spinning.

"I was so confused," Meister told me. "I didn't know what to believe anymore. I began rethinking that vision I had. Maybe it was from Allah or Brahman or some other divine reality. My faith drained away, and I became an agnostic."

He began to seek answers. He was especially helped by a group of Christians he met who gently encouraged him to carefully analyze differing worldviews. *Which is reasonable? Which is logical? Which is livable? Which one has the best evidence on its side?*

He said, "I started at square one by asking, What is truth? I ended up researching worldviews for a year and a half. At the end, the conclusion was clear: Christianity is the most reasonable, the most livable, and the best supported evidentially. And it matched my own personal experiences of God. I recommitted my life to Christ."

After that exhilarating spiritual investigation, he left his engineering career to study theology and philosophy, launching his new calling in teaching others about world religions and the philosophy behind them.

With that background, he has developed what has become known as the Apologetics Pyramid. It illustrates how to evaluate Christianity in a logical and systematic way. The pyramid's goal is not to provide absolute proof, but rather to guide a person's mind toward a reasonable understanding of the evidence about whether Christianity is true.

Meister's pyramid has six layers, and I wanted him to walk me through each one. We started at the base of the pyramid, with the fundamental laws of logic and reality.

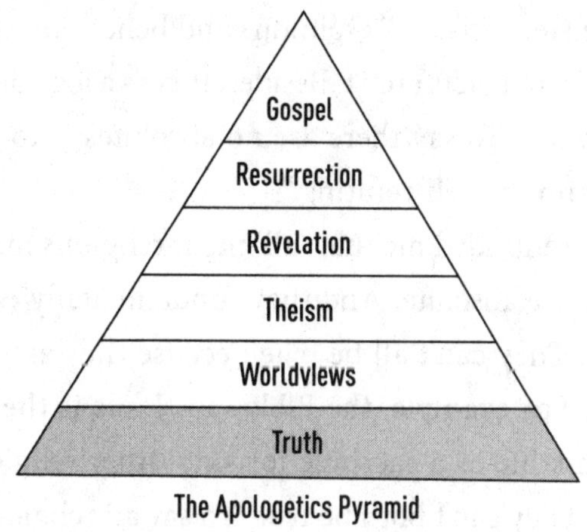

The Apologetics Pyramid

Level 1: Truth—Why Can't Everyone Be Right?

I began our conversation by quoting (from John 18:38) what Pontius Pilate famously asked Jesus: "What is truth?" I asked for Meister's answer to that.

He replied by mentioning something Plato said in ancient Greece—that a true claim states things the way they are, and a false claim states things different from the way they are. "This is the correspondence theory of truth," Meister said. "A claim or proposition is true if it corresponds with facts. And this would mean that truth is absolute and universal."

That of course goes against popular thinking today, which says that truth is relative, not absolute—especially religious truth.

But Meister insisted: "Opinions and beliefs are subjective and personal, but facts aren't. Besides, there's a logical problem with relativism. To say there are no absolutes is to make an absolute claim. It's self-refuting."

He also reminded me that "all major religions make truth claims that are absolute. And they fundamentally contradict each other. They can't all be true because they assert opposite things. For example, the Bible says Jesus is the Messiah who gave his life as a sacrifice for sin. Other religions deny this claim. They can't both be true. To say all religious claims are true may sound respectful and generous, but it's logically absurd. Our task is to discover what's true and what isn't."

"Still, isn't it intolerant to say truth is absolute?"

"Truth can't be bigoted—but people certainly can be,

"All major religions make truth claims that are absolute. And they fundamentally contradict each other. They can't all be true because they assert opposite things. To say all religious claims are true may sound respectful and generous, but it's logically absurd. Our task is to discover what's true and what isn't."

whether they're Christians, atheists, Hindus, or Muslims. Truth is truth, but how we communicate it can be narrow-minded and arrogant. We need to follow the examples of Jesus and Gandhi, who taught in humble though passionate ways."

Level 2: Worldviews—a Three-Way Clash

The next layer of the pyramid examines the three major worldviews.

"A worldview," Meister said, "is a collection of beliefs and ideas about the central issues of life. It's the lens through which we view the world, whether consciously chosen or not.

"Broadly speaking, every religion or ideology can be found within one of three categories—*theism*, *atheism*, or *pantheism*. Since their core assumptions contradict each other, only one of them can be true."

To analyze these worldviews, Meister first asks how each worldview would answer five fundamental questions:

1. Is there a God, and what is God like?
2. What is ultimate reality?
3. How is knowledge obtained?
4. Where is the basis of morality and value found?
5. Who are we as human beings?

Meister asked these questions first about theism, which is belief in a personal God separate from the world.

"For the major theistic religions—Judaism, Christianity, and Islam—there is one God, creator of all, who is all-knowing, all-powerful, all-present, and all-good. The ultimate reality in theism is God, who is beyond the physical realm of existence.

"In theism, we acquire knowledge through our five senses and other means, including the revelation in Scripture.

"The basis of morality in theism is God. Right, wrong, good, evil—they're all based on the nature of the infinite, personal God who created everything.

"Finally, in theism human beings are not on par with God, though we're on a higher plane than the rest of the animal kingdom. We're unique, and we have an immaterial soul that lives on in eternity."

Next he focused on atheism, which of course means disbelief in God or the gods.

"What's the universal reality in atheism? As astronomer Carl Sagan put it [in the 1980 megahit TV series *Cosmos*], 'The universe is all there ever was, is, or will be.' There's no supernatural domain or existence beyond this physical world.

"In atheism, how do we acquire knowledge? Since the physical world is all that exists, any knowledge we have must be about it and it alone. We're limited to empirical knowledge, with the scientific method being the gold standard."

And as for morality: "Atheists don't consider morality to be objectively true. Instead, they typically say it emerged through evolution. In other words, humans—or our genes—invented the idea of morality because it improved our chances for survival, so morality can vary from place to place and time to time.

"Finally, on the question of humankind, atheism says we're electromechanical machines—animals that have grown in complexity over the eons thanks to evolution. There's no soul or immaterial aspect to people. We live, we die, we decay—that's all there is."

Meister's third focus was pantheism, which he said "doesn't have a single form. It has differing philosophical and religious aspects. Generally speaking, there are no ultimate distinctions in the universe—all is changeless, all is one, and all is God—or Brahman, in Hinduism. In short, God is one with the universe.

"As for ultimate reality, it's God—indistinguishable and indescribable. All distinctions are illusions. Animals, plants, insects, rocks, you, me—everything is one and the same fundamental reality.

"For pantheists of this sort, knowledge is acquired not through rational inquiry but through meditation and other practices intended to empty the mind. Chanting and various other techniques are used for altering consciousness and experiencing a unity with all that is.

"Also, objective good and evil are illusory. Morality has no real basis.

"Finally, who are humans? For pantheists, *we* are God; we are spiritual divinity; we are one with the universe. But unfortunately we're under universal illusion, and as a result we don't realize our divine nature. Our goal must therefore be to recognize this truth and win release from this illusion—so we can see and experience the God we really are."

For deciding which of these three worldviews is most plausible, Meister proposed two tests: logic and livability. A worldview is false if its core beliefs are internally contradictory or incoherent. And it should also be rejected if it cannot consistently be lived out.

With atheism, Meister said, "there's the logical problem of good. If morality is a survival mechanism, if it's a mere illusion, it's no more rational to believe in morality than in Santa Claus. It's subjective and relative, not absolute and universal.

"And if there's no objective morality, the atheist can't logically affirm that there are such things as objective good, evil, right, or wrong. An atheist can't even really claim that the murder of innocent children is objectively morally evil. They could say they're offended by it, but that's a preference; they can't consistently affirm it's really wrong.

"If this view of morality were actually lived out, chaos would ensue. Everything would be permitted."

Some atheists have attempted to establish a kind of universal right and wrong, but Meister said these arguments are weak. "If objective moral values exist, then atheistic materialism must be false. Yet objective moral values *do* exist—and we all know it. Therefore, atheistic materialism must be false."

Atheism also fails the livability test. "Atheists cannot consistently live out the view that morality is merely illusory or relative. If someone claimed that killing babies just for fun is okay, nobody would accept that—because we know it is really and truly wrong."

Meister's conclusion therefore is that atheism isn't a reasonable or worthy option.

What about pantheism?

"Pantheists have a problem with right and wrong as well," he said. He told me about having a spaghetti dinner with a pantheist, who told him, "Everything is God and everything is one. There are no distinctions."

"If that's true," Meister told her, "then there's ultimately no right and wrong, no distinction between cruelty and non-cruelty, or between good and evil." With that, he took a pot of boiling water from the stove and held it over her head, pretending he was going to spill it on her. He said teasingly, "Are you *sure* there's no distinction between right and wrong, cruelty and noncruelty?"

She smiled. "Well," she said, "I guess there *does* seem to be a distinction between right and wrong!"

Meister told me, "Pantheists can *say* there's no distinction between good and evil and that suffering is just an illusion—but they can't really live that way.

"Besides," he added, "pantheism seems logically incoherent. In pantheism, I am God and ultimately impersonal. I am the changeless All. Yet I'm told I must discover this fact about myself. Through meditation, I need to realize I am one with the Divine. But I can't be changeless and at the same time change in order to realize that I am changeless.

"Also," he added, "in pantheism the universe is supposed

to be impersonal. But I'm a person with hopes, dreams, thoughts, and feelings—all of which pantheists say are illusions. Somehow the universe coughs up illusory and deceived people, who are really nonpersons, and now they need to get back to the impersonal self that they really are. But if I'm actually an impersonal being, how can I be deceived into believing I'm a personal being who needs to recognize my true, impersonal nature? How can something impersonal be deceived, anyway? It makes no sense.

"Let's face it," Meister said. "If you want to be logical and consistent, pantheism isn't the worldview you want."

So then, what about theism? Doesn't the existence of evil and suffering invalidate theism? Isn't it a contradiction to say there's a God who's powerful and loving, yet evil exists in the world he created?

"That's a serious problem," Meister acknowledged. "I don't pretend it isn't. But it's not unique to theism. All worldviews wrestle with the issue of evil and suffering. For theism, however, I don't believe it's a contradiction. In fact, I'd say Christians have the most plausible response.

"For one thing, it's at least logically plausible to say that if there's a God, he gave people free will." He said that the very notion of moral responsibility and the ability to do good requires freedom. "Even love requires the freedom to choose *not* to love—which is why robots can't fall in love. They can only do what they're programmed to do.

"God could have created a world where people were like robots, but then we could never experience the highest value in the universe, which is love. We couldn't truly be doing actions that are good and moral. And where there's freedom, this necessarily involves the freedom to turn against the good. That's a plausible explanation for why we have moral evil in the world."

He added that God is able to take even bad and harmful things that happen and use them for our good. "The Bible talks about how hardship develops character and perseverance [as in Romans 5:3–4, for example]. Sometimes it takes trials and tribulations to make us into mature, spiritual human beings. We all know that if we raise children in a totally sheltered way, they won't fully mature. Now, we can resist God and become hardened against him, but that's not what he wants."

Meister continued: "There's no contradiction in God existing and evil existing—if God has a good and sufficient reason for allowing evil to exist. As I've shown, it's at least logically possible that God does have such reasons."

So for Meister, pantheism and atheism are disqualified, but theism isn't.

"Given all this," he said, "my conclusion is that theism in general—and Christianity in particular—seem to be the most plausible worldview."

Level 3: Theism—the Fingerprints of God

I was interested in hearing more evidence for theism. So I offered Meister a challenge: "Give me three positive reasons that theism is true."

He first brought up the fine-tuning of the universe, and also how the beginning of the universe points powerfully toward a creator. The third reason he gave was the so-called moral argument, which he now spelled out in its most basic form.

"If there are objective moral values, then God exists," he said. "Objective moral values are precepts that are universally binding on all people at all times and places, whether they follow them or not. And we know that objective moral values *do* exist—for example, that it's objectively evil to torture a baby for fun. Therefore, God exists."

Again he concluded, "For these and many other reasons, I'm convinced that theism is the most plausible worldview—by a long shot."

That brought us to the next level of the pyramid.

Level 4: Revelation—Has God Spoken to Humankind?

But which "brand" of theism rings true?

Every major religion believes its scriptures have authority and are divinely inspired. Christians see no conflict between their New Testament and the Jewish scriptures contained in the Old Testament, since Christians regard their faith as being the fulfillment of Judaism. However, the differences between the Christian Bible and other sacred texts cannot be reconciled.

For example, the Qur'an explicitly contradicts biblical

"If there are objective moral values, then God exists. Objective moral values are precepts that are universally binding on all people at all times and places, whether they follow them or not. And we know that objective moral values *do* exist—for example, that it's objectively evil to torture a baby for fun. Therefore, God exists."

teaching about the Trinity, the death and resurrection of Jesus, and Jesus as God's unique Son. Consequently, if it's plausible to believe that the Bible is reliable, this rules out the claims in the Qur'an that contradict those in the Bible.

I asked Meister how we can test whether the New Testament can be trusted.

He said that the first issue would be deciding whether we can trust how the New Testament text was passed down through history. "It's no exaggeration to say the evidence for the New Testament text is staggering. We have more than 5,800 ancient Greek manuscripts and fragments, some of which date back to less than a hundred years after the originals. That swamps other ancient writings. While this information doesn't prove the New Testament is true, it does offer good reason to believe we have a reasonably accurate representation of what was originally written."

Although there are sometimes differences in how a certain passage appears in various manuscripts, Meister said that the vast majority of the variations are minor spelling differences. He said that no core doctrine of Christianity was at stake.

Next, Meister mentioned how often the New Testament refers to its content coming from eyewitnesses to the events. "No other religious text has this level of eyewitness authentication," he said. "That gives the New Testament special credibility."

He spoke also of the outside sources that support what we see in the New Testament. "Over and over, archaeological discoveries have confirmed—and never disproven—core New

Testament references. Plus, there are ancient writings outside the Bible that corroborate the basic outline of Jesus's life."

His conclusion: "Any reasonable person would be justified in deciding that the Bible is essentially trustworthy."

Level 5: Resurrection—Did Jesus Rise from the Grave?

The next category of evidence for Christianity, Meister said, is the resurrection of Jesus, which vindicated his claim to being the Messiah and God's unique Son (Jesus himself made this claim in John 10:30).

Meister said, "Many books have been written to refute the naturalistic explanations that skeptics have put forward. The historical facts, in my opinion, are convincing—Jesus rose from the grave and, in doing so, demonstrated his divine nature.

"And this clinches Christianity as the worldview that makes the most sense to me. It's plausible and it's livable."

As Meister's apologetics pyramid demonstrates, Christianity is built on a solid foundation that can be trusted. In fact, Meister added, "through the years, a lot of people who started out as doubters have become believers after studying the evidence."

At the Top: The Gospel—Opening Heaven's Door

The summit of the pyramid is the good news of the gospel. Logic and evidence narrow the credible choices down to one option: Jesus and his freely offered gift of forgiveness and eternal life. As Jesus said in Luke 4:43, "I must proclaim the good news of the kingdom of God . . . because that is why I was sent."

What is the good news? That Jesus is the Messiah who was unjustly killed, was resurrected in triumph over death, ascended to the Father, and is coming back to rule. Indeed, his death and resurrection were for *us*. He died to pay the penalty we deserved for our sins, and he rose to open the gates of heaven for all who come to him in repentance and faith.

It's an amazing truth. The God we sinned against loved us enough to sacrifice the life of his only Son, to adopt us as his children, and to invite us to spend eternity with him.

"Jesus opens God's kingdom to us," Meister said. "The kingdom of God is where God rules in a perfect way—he loves his people, provides for them, cares for them—and we gratefully love and serve and worship him in return. He invites everybody to enter—and in his kingdom, we are transformed."

The credibility of Christianity demonstrated by Chad Meister's apologetics pyramid gives us confidence that the Christian version of the afterlife is the only one that passes the tests of logic and evidence.

Still, for many people a couple of roadblocks stand in the way. We'll explore these challenges in the chapters that follow.

CHAPTER 7

CHALLENGE #1—IF GOD IS REAL, WHY IS THERE SUFFERING?

Hardships. Betrayal. Illness. Injury. Heartbreak. Everyone suffers, to some degree.

Why? *Why?*

This isn't merely an intellectual issue; it's an intensely personal matter that can tie our emotions into knots and leave us with spiritual vertigo—disoriented, frightened, and angry.

And it appears to be the single biggest obstacle for spiritual seekers. I once sponsored a national survey that said, "If you could ask God only one question and you knew he would give you an answer right now, what would you ask?" By a long shot, the top response was this: "Why is there pain and suffering in the world?"

This question, in short, is humanity's heart cry.

But does the presence of suffering necessarily mean the absence of God?

To explore this matter, I met in Boston with the author of *Making Sense out of Suffering*—a book whose title summed up exactly what I was seeking to do.

Peter Kreeft, PhD, is a first-rate philosopher. He earned a doctorate from Fordham University, did postgraduate study at Yale University, and has several decades of experience as a professor at Villanova University and Boston College. And he's written or coauthored more than eighty books, including *Love Is Stronger Than Death* and *Jesus Shock*. Yet he's no stuffy academic. He has a winsome and engaging manner.

What drew me to Kreeft were his insights in *Making Sense out of Suffering*. In that book he skillfully weaves a journey of discovery. The clues along the way finally converge on Jesus and the tears of God.

A Bear, a Trap, a Hunter, and God

I began by confronting Kreeft head-on with the burning issue: How could a loving God allow evil? How is that even possible?

Kreeft focused first on that word *possible*. He called it "intellectually arrogant" to insist there's *no* possibility that a loving God— "who knows far more than we do, including about our future"—could possibly tolerate the extreme evil and suffering we see in history and in today's world. He proposed a "somewhat more reasonable position." He said there's at least "a small possibility" that a loving God allows this. "How can a mere finite human be sure that infinite wisdom would not tolerate certain short-range evils in order for longer-range good that we couldn't foresee?"

He then asked me a surprising question. "Would you agree that the difference between us and God is greater than the difference between us and, say, a bear?"

I agreed. He gave me a story to illustrate a point.

"Imagine a bear in a trap. A hunter comes along, and out of sympathy he wants to liberate the bear. He tries to win the bear's confidence, but he can't. So he has to shoot the bear full of drugs. The bear, however, thinks this is an attack—that the hunter is trying to kill him.

"Then in order to get the bear out of the trap, the hunter has to push him further *into* the trap to release the tension on the spring. If the bear is semiconscious at this point, he's even more convinced that the hunter is his enemy, wanting to cause him suffering and pain. But the bear would be wrong. The bear reaches this incorrect conclusion because he's not a human being like the hunter."

Kreeft continued, "I believe God does the same with us sometimes. And we can't comprehend why, any more than the bear can understand the hunter's motivations. As the bear could have trusted the hunter—so we can trust God."

For and Against God

Kreeft understands why people question God's goodness in the face of evil and suffering all around. He says they're responding "in a very honest and heartfelt way to the fact that *something counts against God*. Only in a world where faith is difficult can faith exist. I don't have faith in two plus two equals four or in the noonday sun. Those are beyond question. But Scripture describes God as a hidden God. You have to make an effort of faith to find him. There are clues you can follow."

He said that if there were no such clues, "it's difficult for me to understand how we could really be free to make a choice about him. If we had absolute proof instead of clues, then you could no more deny God than you could deny the sun. If we had no evidence at all, you could never get there. God gives us just enough evidence so that those who *want* him can have him. Those who want to follow the clues will unlock them."

He quoted words of Jesus (from Matthew 7:7): "*Seek and you will find*. It doesn't say everybody will find him; it doesn't say nobody will find him. But some *will find*. Who? Those who *seek*—those whose hearts are set on finding him, and who follow the clues."

I asked Kreeft to clarify what he meant in saying earlier that "something counts against God"—that evil and suffering are evidence against him. Was Kreeft conceding that evil disproves God's existence?

"No," he insisted. "I'm saying that in this world there is

evidence against and evidence for God. There's no question that the existence of evil is one argument against God." He noted that in his book *Handbook of Christian Apologetics* (coauthored with Ronald K. Tacelli), he summarizes twenty arguments "that point persuasively in the other direction—in favor of the existence of God. Atheists must answer all twenty arguments; theists must answer only one. However, each of us gets to cast our vote."

Evil as Evidence for God

Kreeft then startled me with this remark: "Besides, the evidence of evil and suffering can actually be used in *favor* of God."

He explained that when people respond to evil with outrage, "it presupposes that there really is a difference between good and evil." We use the standard of good to judge evil—to say that suffering isn't what *ought* to be. We understand what ought to be, "and that this notion corresponds to something real, and that there is, therefore, a reality called the Supreme Good—another name for God."

Kreeft said his point was this: "If there is no God, where did we get the standard of goodness by which we judge evil as evil?"

He added that the very presence in our minds of these ideas of evil and goodness is something that "needs to be accounted for"—and that atheism fails to do that.

Atheism, he said, "is a *cheap* answer. Atheism is cheap on people. How is it possible that more than 90 percent of all the human beings who have ever lived—usually in far more painful circumstances than we—could believe in God? The objective evidence, just looking at the balance of pleasure and suffering in the world, would *not* seem to justify believing in an absolutely good God. Yet this has been almost universally believed. Are they all crazy?

"Also, atheism robs death of meaning. And if death has no meaning, how can life ultimately have meaning? Atheism cheapens everything it touches.

"And in the end, when the atheist dies and encounters God instead of the nothingness they had predicted, they'll recognize that atheism was a cheap answer because it refused the only thing that's not cheap—the God of infinite value."

A Problem of Logic

Our conversation went deeper.

Kreeft mentioned that Christians believe these five things: (1) God exists; (2) God is all-good; (3) God is all-powerful; (4) God is all-wise; and (5) evil exists. But how could all those statements be true at the same time?

"It seems," he said, "you have to drop one of those beliefs. If God is all-powerful, he can do anything. If God is all-good, he wants only good. If God is all-wise, he knows what is good. So if all those beliefs are true—and Christians believe they

"How is it possible that more than 90 percent of all the human beings who have ever lived—usually in far more painful circumstances than we—could believe in God? The objective evidence, just looking at the balance of pleasure and suffering in the world, would *not* seem to justify believing in an absolutely good God. Yet this has been almost universally believed. Are they all crazy?"

are—then it would seem that the consequence is that no evil can exist."

But of course, evil *does* exist. Was it then logical to assume that an all-good, all-powerful, all-wise God doesn't exist?

"I'd say one of those beliefs about him must be false," Kreeft said, "or we're not understanding it in the right way."

So we explored the logic further.

God as All-Powerful

Kreeft explained that to say God is all-powerful means "he can do everything that is meaningful, everything that is possible, everything that makes any sense at all. God cannot make himself cease to exist. He cannot make good evil."

So there are some things God *can't* do?

Kreeft went on, "Precisely *because* he is all-powerful, he can't make mistakes. Only weak and stupid beings make mistakes. One such mistake would be to try to create a self-contradiction—like two plus two equals five, or a round square.

"Now, the classic defense of God against the problem of evil is that it's not logically possible to have free will and no possibility of moral evil. In other words, once God chose to create human beings with free will, it was up to them—rather than up to God—as to whether there was sin or not. That's what free will means. Built into the situation of God deciding to create human beings is the chance of evil, and consequently the suffering that results."

Then did God *create* evil?

"God created the *possibility* of evil," Kreeft said. "The source of evil is not God's power, but rather mankind's freedom. Even an all-powerful God could not have created a world in which people had genuine freedom and yet there was no potential for sin, because our freedom includes the possibility of sin within its own meaning. To ask why God didn't create a world where there's real choice but no possibility of choosing evil is like asking why God didn't create colorless color or round squares."

So why didn't God create a world *without* human freedom?

Such a world, Kreeft said, would have to be a world without humans. "Would it have been a place without suffering? Yes. But also a world without love, which is the highest value in the universe. Real love—our love of God and our love of each other—must involve a choice. But granting that choice brings the possibility that people will choose instead to hate."

Kreeft noted that God created a world he called "good" (as we read in Genesis), where people were free to choose to love God or turn away from him. "That potential for sin was actualized not by God, but by people. The blame, ultimately, lies with us. He did his part perfectly; we're the ones who messed up."

God as All-Knowing

"If God is all-wise," Kreeft continued, "he knows not only the present but also the future. He knows not only present good and evil but also future good and evil. If his wisdom vastly exceeds ours, it is at least possible that a loving God could deliberately tolerate horrible things like starvation because he foresees that in the long run, more people will be better and happier than if he miraculously intervened. That's at least intellectually possible."

But was this idea a cop-out?

Kreeft put it to the test. "God has clearly shown us how this can work. He has demonstrated how the very worst thing that has ever happened in the history of the world ended up resulting in the very best thing that has ever happened in the history of the world. I'm referring to the death of God himself on the cross.

"At the time, nobody saw how anything good could result from this tragedy. And yet God foresaw that the result would be the opening of heaven to human beings. So the worst tragedy in history brought about the most glorious event in history. And if it happened there—if the ultimate evil can result in the ultimate good—it can happen elsewhere, even in our own individual lives."

He said that the suffering Christ endured on the cross "is literally unimaginable. It's not just what you and I would have experienced in our own finite human agony, physical and mental, but all the sufferings of the world were there. Just imagine every single pain in the history of the world all rolled together into a ball, eaten by God, digested, and fully tasted—eternally.

"The fact that he went beyond justice and quite incredibly took all the suffering upon himself makes him so winsome that the answer to suffering is this: How could you not love this Being who went the extra mile, who practiced more than he preached, who entered into our world, who suffered our pains, who offers himself to us in the midst of our sorrows? What more could he do?

"God's answer to the problem of suffering is that *he came right down into it.* Many Christians try to get God off the hook for suffering. But God put himself on the hook, so to speak—on the cross."

Kreeft came to this practical conclusion: "If we want to be with God, we have to be with suffering. We have to not avoid the cross, either in thought or in fact. We must go where *he* is, and the cross is one of the places where he is. When he sends us the sunrises, we thank him for the sunrises; when he sends us sunsets—and death and suffering and crosses—we also thank him for that."

He added that thanking God for the pain that befalls us is something we'll do in heaven. "We will say to God, 'Thank you so much for the times of pain I didn't understand back then. I now see that these were such precious things in my life.'

"Seeing the face of God, the good of God, the joy of God—the God available to all who seek him in the midst of their pain—will infinitely outweigh all the sufferings and even the joys of this world.

"I think any fairly mature Christian can even now look back on their life and identify some moment of suffering that made them much closer to God than they ever thought possible.

"And compared with knowing God eternally—that

intimacy with God—nothing else counts. That's what's going to satisfy us forever in heaven.

"As we look at human relationships, what we see is that lovers don't want explanations, but rather *presence*. And what God is, essentially, is presence. The doctrine of the Trinity says God is three persons who are present to one another in perfect knowledge and perfect love. That's why God is infinite joy. As we participate in that presence, we too have infinite joy."

God as All-Good

We looked next at God's attribute of goodness.

"*Good* is a tricky word," Kreeft began, "because even in human affairs there's such a wide range of meaning. But the fact that God deliberately allows certain things that hurt us doesn't necessarily count against God."

He explained his meaning: "It's at least possible that God is wise enough to foresee how we need some pain for reasons we may not understand, but which he foresees as being necessary toward some eventual good. Therefore, he's not being evil by allowing that pain to exist.

"Dentists, athletic trainers, teachers, parents—they all know that sometimes to be good is *not* to be kind. Certainly, there are times when God allows suffering and deprives us of the lesser good of pleasure in order to help us toward the greater good of moral and spiritual education. We know that moral character gets formed through hardship, through overcoming obstacles, through enduring despite difficulties. Courage, for example, would be impossible in a world without pain.

"Let's face it, we learn from the mistakes we make and the suffering they bring. The universe is a soul-making machine, and part of that process is learning, maturing, and growing through difficult and challenging and painful experiences. The point of our lives in this world isn't comfort but rather training and preparation for eternity."

Kreeft stated his belief that all suffering contains at least the opportunity for good. "Just about every human being can reflect on their past and say, 'I learned from that hardship.' Even people without religious faith are aware of this dimension of suffering. But not all of us learn and benefit from suffering; that's where free will comes in."

He raised the question of what human beings would be like if our world had no suffering. "Impossibly spoiled little brats," he said. "That's what we'd become."

"In fact, to prevent all evil, you must remove all freedom and reduce people to puppets—with no ability to freely choose love."

Kreeft mentioned also how human suffering can lead to repentance for sin before God—a result we observe historically in the Bible. "And repentance leads to something wonderful—to blessedness, since God is the source of all joy and all life. The outcome is good—in fact, better than good.

"And pain and suffering are frequently the means by which we become motivated to finally surrender to God and seek the cure of Christ. That's what we need most desperately. That's what will bring us the supreme joy of knowing Jesus. The great Christians from history will tell you that this result is worth *any* suffering."

"Let's face it, we learn from the mistakes we make and the suffering they bring. The universe is a soul-making machine, and part of that process is learning, maturing, and growing through difficult and challenging and painful experiences. The point of our lives in this world isn't comfort but rather training and preparation for eternity."

More Questions

Kreeft was shedding light on the mystery of suffering. But each new insight seemed to spawn new questions.

I mentioned to him how evil people get away with hurting others all the time. "Certainly, God can't consider that fair," I said. "Why doesn't he intervene?"

"People *aren't* getting away with it," Kreeft replied. "Justice delayed is not necessarily justice denied. There will come a day when God will settle accounts. People will be held responsible for the evil they've perpetrated and the suffering they've caused. Criticizing God for not doing it right now is like reading half a novel and criticizing the author for not resolving the plot.

"God will bring accountability at the right time. In fact, the Bible says [as in 2 Peter 3:9] that one reason he's delaying this judgment is that some people are still following the clues. They have yet to find him. He's actually delaying the end of history out of his great love for these people."

But what about the sheer amount of suffering in the world? I asked Kreeft, "Couldn't God curtail at least some of the more horrific evil?"

He took me back to the core question of our discussion: Does evil's existence disprove God's existence? If this is a quantity issue—then how much is too much or too little? He indicated that suffering doesn't fit into that kind of analysis. "At what point," he asked, "does suffering disprove the existence of God? No such point can be shown. Besides, because we're not God, we can't say how much suffering is needed."

Helping Others Who Suffer

Kreeft gestured toward the hallway and said, "On my door there's a cartoon of two turtles. One says, 'Sometimes I'd like to ask God why he allows poverty, famine, and injustice, when he could do something about it.' The other turtle says, 'I'm afraid God might ask me the same question.'

"Those who have Jesus's heart toward hurting people need to live out their faith by alleviating suffering where they can, by making a difference, by showing his love in practical ways."

Kreeft said that the first thing we must do with other people who are suffering is to listen to them, to be aware of them, and to see and feel their pain. "The thing to do with pain is to enter it, and then you learn something from it." He said this makes it possible for us to truly minister to the suffering—to love, comfort, embrace, and weep with them. "Our love—a reflection of God's love—should spur us to help others who are hurting."

God, Where Are You?

I could sense an increasing passion and conviction in Kreeft's voice. In summing up our conversation, Kreeft shared with me that the answer to suffering "is the Answerer. It's Jesus himself. It's not a bunch of words; it's *the* Word. It's not a tightly woven philosophical argument. It's a person. *The* person.

"The answer to suffering cannot just be an abstract idea,

because this isn't an abstract issue. It's a personal issue. It requires a personal response. The answer must be some*one*, not just some*thing*. Because the issue involves Someone: *God, where are you?*"

He continued: "Jesus is there, sitting beside us in the lowest places of our lives. Are we broken? *He* was broken, like pieces of bread from the loaf, for us. Are we despised? *He* was despised and rejected by men. Do we cry out that we can't take any more? *He* was a man of sorrows and acquainted with grief. Do people betray us? *He* was sold out himself. Are our tenderest relationships broken? *He*, too, loved and was rejected. Do people turn from us? *He* was one from whom people hid their faces as though he were a leper.

"Does he descend into the hells of each one of us? Yes, he does. And Jesus not only rose from the dead; he changed the meaning of death and therefore of all the little deaths—the sufferings that anticipate death and show all the aspects of it."

Kreeft said slowly, "In the end, God has given us only partial explanations. Maybe that's because he saw that a better explanation wouldn't have been good for us. I don't know why. As a philosopher, I'm obviously curious. Humanly, I wish he had given us more information.

"But he knew that Jesus was more than an explanation. *He's what we really need.* If your friend is sick and dying, the most important thing he wants is not an explanation; he wants you to sit with him. He's terrified of being alone more than anything else. So God has not left us alone."

He leaned back and said, "And for that, *I love him.*"

[illegible]

[illegible] continued. [illegible] sitting beside [illegible] in the [illegible] est places of our lives. [illegible] and [illegible] [illegible] [illegible] [illegible] forgot. [illegible] what we [illegible] [illegible] questions and [illegible] [illegible] [illegible] [illegible] [illegible] [illegible] [illegible] [illegible] [illegible] had [illegible] a leg.

[illegible] the [illegible] [illegible] and [illegible] [illegible] [illegible] [illegible] [illegible] [illegible]

[illegible] [illegible] [illegible] [illegible] [illegible] unknown information.

[illegible] [illegible] explanation [illegible] [illegible] [illegible]

He [illegible]

[illegible]

CHAPTER 8

CHALLENGE #2—IF GOD IS REAL, WHY IS HE SO HIDDEN?

Why doesn't God make his existence much more obvious? Obvious enough that no rational person could doubt that he's real.

If God is truly loving and wants a relationship with humankind—wouldn't he make certain that every person who isn't actively resisting him would always have a solid belief in him?

Provocative questions indeed. To investigate, I reached out to a respected and widely published author whose entire career has been devoted to responding to troublesome questions about faith.

Kenneth Samples began to seek answers to deep questions in his life after a family tragedy. His brother Frank—who had plummeted into despair after struggling with drug addiction and incarceration—ended his own life.

That suicide rocked Kenneth's world. He started wondering: *What do I have in my life that's really meaningful?*

His spiritual curiosity had already been stirred up when his sister gave him a copy of *Mere Christianity* by C. S. Lewis. Later he had a vivid dream in which he encountered a Christlike figure with scars and bruises on his face.

"When he spoke, it was like *thunder*," Samples told me. This resulted in an insatiable urge to study the Bible and attend church.

He became a committed Christian and immediately gravitated toward apologetics. He earned an undergraduate degree in history from Concordia University, then a master's degree in theological studies from Biola University.

Samples worked for a time alongside Walter Martin, a legendary countercult apologist. Samples now serves as senior research scholar for Reasons to Believe, a nonprofit educational center that focuses on science and faith. For more than twenty years, he has taught at Biola and lectured at universities around the country. His books include *Without a Doubt: Answering the 20 Toughest Faith Questions* and *Christianity Cross-Examined: Is It Rational, Relevant, and Good?*

There are virtually no objections to Christianity that he hasn't addressed over his career.

God's Silence Through the Centuries

As I met with Samples, I began by mentioning several theists in history who struggled with the apparent silence of God, yet did not abandon their faith. In the Psalms, for example, Israel's King David calls out, "My God, my God, why have you forsaken me? . . . I cry out by day, but you do not answer, by night, but I find no rest" (22:1–2). In the Bible we also read these words spoken to the Lord by the prophet Isaiah: "Truly you are a God who has been hiding himself" (Isaiah 45:15).

These passages of Scripture (and others like them) seem to indicate that feeling distant from God was not uncommon for his worshipers in ancient Israel. Nevertheless, as they experienced the sorrow of this distance, they did not appear to question God's reality.

I asked Samples, "Why do you think that many theists have struggled with the so-called hiddenness of God, yet did not give up their belief in him?"

Samples began his answer by defining faith as "a confident trust in a reliable source. We put our faith in something that's reliable. By that definition, faith has a rational component to it."

He continued. "These individuals put their trust in the one true God, someone they determined to be reliable and trustworthy. It was a faith that made sense and was fully rational. Of course, as C. S. Lewis said [in *Mere Christianity*], you have to feed your faith. I believe they did that. And they ended up building a robust and resilient faith that could withstand the times when they felt perplexed by the seeming absence of God."

"How did they feed their faith?" I asked.

"Through regular prayer, the study of Scripture, being part of a faith community, for example. When you invest in your faith that way, it can sustain you even during those times when God seems distant."

He added, "Sometimes when I talk to people who have walked away from faith, I ask them about their prayer life and their connection to a church—and there isn't anything there. Without that firm foundation, a person's faith can crumble during times when God seems particularly distant. I know in my own life that when God appears hidden, it's often when I'm at a spiritual low."

"Put Your House in Order"

I asked Samples if he ever felt frustrated because God wasn't making himself more real.

"Yes," he said. He described a time at age forty-five when he became sick, then was told he had contracted a rare bacteria that had severely damaged his right lung and his brain. His doctor gave him an 80 percent chance of dying from this. Samples said that when he heard this report, "a cold breeze ran through my soul. I ended up going through a difficult period."

He was hospitalized and had lung surgery. "Through it all, there certainly were times when God seemed present, and that was comforting. But then one night, my family and friends went home from the hospital and I couldn't sleep. I thought, *Lord, where are you? I'm in a tough spot.*"

"Did the silence of God threaten your faith?"

"Not in a serious way. As I began to think more clearly, I fell back on some things I had learned through the years."

"For instance?"

"I realized that this experience of God's silence didn't invalidate the fact that I had encountered God before. And it certainly didn't rule out the solid arguments I'd discovered about God's existence and the truth of Christianity. So, yes, there were times when I thought, *Lord, where are you?* And that can be scary. But when I fell back on the spiritual practices that I had nurtured through the years—prayer and worship, for example—the dark thoughts dissipated. Just reading the Gospels raised my spirits."

"Were you concerned you might die?"

"I remember the doctor saying to me, 'Hey, put your house in order.' I started asking myself, *What do I really believe about life after death?* That prompted me to go through all the evidence for the resurrection that I had researched through the years. I realized that the evidence was sound when I first came across it, and it remained sound, and I trusted that it would continue to be sound into the future."

"In the end, did this experience make you more sympathetic to people who wrestle with the silence of God?"

"Absolutely," he replied. "I can relate to what they're going through. And yet at the same time, can we really say that God has been hidden—when the second person of the Trinity took on a human nature and entered into our world? I've found that just bringing that to mind has been an encouragement to me."

The Pitcher and the Catcher

One reason I sought out Samples was that he had written and published an article on the hiddenness of God. In the article, he used a metaphor from baseball. As a former catcher who once aspired to the Major Leagues, Samples drew on his athletic background to look into the charge that God's hiddenness disproves his existence.

The atheist argument basically says that if a loving God existed, he would make himself so clearly known to humankind that no rational person could doubt his existence. But there are people who are open to believing in God and yet aren't convinced he's real. Therefore, this shows that a loving God doesn't actually exist—so the argument goes.

Samples then gave his baseball illustration. In baseball, the pitcher is the sender, and the catcher is the receiver. God is like the pitcher, and we—human beings—are like the catcher. So when we aren't receiving the evidence of God's existence, who's at fault—pitcher or catcher?

Is there some problem with the pitcher? Is God failing to send adequate evidence of his existence to humankind? Or is there a problem with the catcher? Are there specific reasons why we, as human beings, aren't receiving the evidence?

"From a biblical view," Samples said, "I would argue that

"Can we really say that God has been hidden—when the second person of the Trinity took on a human nature and entered into our world? I've found that just bringing that to mind has been an encouragement to me."

there's a stronger case for the failure resting with the receiver rather than the sender. At the forefront of Jewish and Christian religion is the idea that God has revealed himself. He does that through two books—the book of nature and the Bible. The book of nature supports the book of Scripture, while the book of Scripture explains the book of nature."

"Define what you mean by the book of nature."

"The universe is like a storehouse of knowledge, so it's similar to a book. You can get information or knowledge from it. We call this general revelation."

"And what is nature's essential message?"

"In the Old Testament, Psalm 19 begins this way: 'The heavens declare the glory of God; the skies proclaim the work of his hands. Day after day they pour forth speech; night after night they reveal knowledge.' This passage indicates that the universe is continually pointing toward God's existence. It's perpetual; it hasn't stopped. It's going on today, and it will continue tomorrow. We can see that the heavens are glorious and complex, and this points toward a creator."

He also gave a New Testament example. "Romans 1:20 says that from the evidence of nature, we can discern 'God's invisible qualities'—in particular, 'his eternal power and divine nature.' In fact, this verse says that God's existence can be '*clearly* seen' by everyone, 'so that people are without excuse.' This is a powerful passage. And in Romans 2, we see that we have a conscience, which is held captive before a moral God."

He went on, "The problem comes because we're sinners. Our natural tendency is to rebel against God and to 'suppress the truth' (Romans 1:18). This suppression is like a pedal—we push it down, and the awareness of God pops it up. But we keep pushing it down again. So I would say that the problem is our own spiritual insensitivity or self-imposed spiritual blindness. One of the destructive effects of sin is that it blinds people from seeing their spiritual and moral failings and their accountability before God."

I told Samples, "Atheists however would say some people are neutral. They're truly open to believing in God—they're willing to believe—and yet they don't or can't."

He responded, "But the Bible's insights into our human nature tell us that no one is really neutral. Nobody is totally without bias. We all have predispositions and presuppositions. As sinners, our natural tendency apart from God's grace is to deflect our moral responsibility before God. We don't want to be held accountable by him, so we suppress the truth about his existence.

"Our inclination is to turn away from him. It's not just that we're blind; we're *willfully* blind. So I would challenge the idea that anyone is in a neutral position. We're not as detached and coolly objective as some intellectuals and atheists would like to think."

C-L-E-A-R Evidence for God

Samples went on to speak of "cumulative" evidence for God's existence—based on careful reasoning. "We see our world and ask, What is the best explanation for it? I use letters from the word *clear* to summarize it.

"The *C* is for cosmos—we have a fine-tuned universe that had a beginning, and this points toward a creator.

"The *L* is for life—the Christian story has uncanny insights into our lives, our challenges, our longings, and our neediness.

"The *E* is for ethics—we live in an ethical world. There are universal moral laws and commands. Where do they come from? Evolution cannot account for that.

"The *A* is for abstractions. These are invisible ideas. We can't have science without mathematics. We can't have philosophy without logic. Again, where do these come from?

"And the *R* is for religion—we all seem to be oriented toward religion, and Christianity provides a strong case that Jesus is the God we need."

I asked Samples, "What about people who say they've tried their best to sincerely seek God, but haven't found him yet?"

He replied, "I would repeat the words of Jesus [from Matthew 7:7]: Keep seeking, asking, and knocking. Just because you haven't found faith yet doesn't mean you never will. But I might also ask, What are your presuppositions? What would God have to do in order for you to accept him? What would you consider to be real evidence? Are there any under-the-surface reasons why you secretly don't want to find him?"

He added, "And I'd quote French philosopher Blaise Pascal's advice to some of his friends: If you can't seem to have faith, why don't you do what people with faith do? Why don't you pray? If there's no God, it's not going to hurt you. Why don't you open the Bible and read what religious people read? Why don't you go to church and see what's going on there? When you are around people who believe, who pray, and who are reading Scripture—who knows what benefits you might derive?"

Samples continued: "We have to come to God on *his* terms, not ours. That means humility rather than pride; it means repentance rather than sinfulness; it means confession and submission. I wonder how many people who say they're open to God would really come to him only if they could do it on their own terms. Frankly, they want God to come to them rather than them coming to him."

I pointed out that there have been times in history when God has made his existence glaringly obvious, such as when he guided the Israelites through the desert and parted the Red Sea. Yet even that didn't produce lasting heart change in people. Israel still fell into spiritual rebellion.

"Why should we think that people would react any differently if he made his existence even more obvious today?" I asked.

"That's a good point. To have faith, the mind has to obtain knowledge, but the will has to be engaged and the heart needs to trust. It's one thing to know some historical facts about Jesus; it's quite another to receive him as our forgiver and leader, and to make a commitment of the will to follow him."

Samples also mentioned the value of hardships in turning us toward God. "The things that have really changed my life for the positive are almost always the trials, difficulties, and problems I've encountered. Our struggles can lead us to deeper study and more honest and heartfelt prayers. Even when I've experienced challenges to my faith, it has caused me to look for God even harder. Romans 8:28 assures us that 'in all things God works for the good of those who love him, who have been called according to his purpose.'

"The great news is that God can cause our struggles to bring about good—a more profound faith, a more devout faith, a better-tested faith, a faith that has been purified by the fire of doubt."

Samples took a moment to summarize what we'd discussed so far. "God has provided sufficient evidence of his existence, but the problem lies with us. Humans have misused their freedom by rebelling against God. And apart from receiving God's saving grace, they naturally suppress the truth of God and their moral responsibility before him. So biblically speaking, the denial of God's existence isn't because of God's absence or hiddenness. Rather, it stems from moral and spiritual insensitivity and blindness that has resulted from our fallen nature and our spiritually resistant condition."

Actual Problems with the Pitcher?

There was one more facet of divine hiddenness I wanted to explore. I returned to the analogy of the pitcher and catcher in baseball. Could some big failure actually be possible on the

"The great news is that God can cause our struggles to bring about good—a more profound faith, a more devout faith, a better tested faith, a faith that has been purified by the fire of doubt."

part of the sender, the pitcher? In other words, couldn't there be a problem with God himself?

Samples answered, "Part of the weakness in this idea is that we tend to view God as just being a magnified version of ourselves," Samples said. "But he's far more otherworldly than that. That means our encounters with God are going to involve some degree of mystery. We have to consider the possibility that he has reasons for his apparent silence that we just can't comprehend."

He added, "Christianity is a reasonable faith, but let's not forget it's still faith." He said God may seem silent at times, but the reason is our own inability to grasp what he's up to in our lives.

"For people who aren't really serious about encountering him, perhaps God chooses to be distant. For those who are sincerely looking for him, he might make himself more evident. And keep in mind that God is omniscient. If that's true, we can assume that he would know how much to reveal about himself to each person—so that the maximum number of people will come into a saving relationship with him."

As we closed our discussion, Samples added this: "When I was going through that life-threatening health crisis, I would have loved a closer personal encounter with God—to have him tangibly appear to me, to have him hold my hand, to have him embrace me and reassure me. Who wouldn't want that? But it didn't happen.

"But what *did* happen," he continued, "is that I was able to fall back on all the reasons for the existence of God that I had encountered in my years of study. God may at times appear hidden and he may seem silent, but that doesn't rule out these theistic arguments that have been around for centuries. And those things encouraged and sustained me when I was sick."

"Have you ever thought about what would have happened if you had died?" I asked.

Samples smiled. "That's the ironic part. If I had, then the hiddenness of God would have been solved for me forever. Because Scripture tells me I would have encountered God face to face. Now, that may well be a metaphor, but it points to an encouraging truth: When any follower of Jesus passes from this world, they enter into an eternal existence where there's intimacy with God on a breathtaking level.

"We will enjoy him and revel in him and worship him and serve him forever in a joyful and exhilarating place called heaven. We'll experience him in a profoundly personal way. I've been longing for that my whole life—and because God is real, I have confidence it will come to pass. And that gives the hiddenness of God a whole different perspective."

[illegible]

"Have you ever thought [illegible]

[illegible]

[illegible]

[illegible]

CONCLUSION

Your Own Encounter with the Real God

In this book, you've pondered evidence for deciding whether God is real. You've digested facts. You've read reports of people's personal experiences with God. You've considered arguments for and against.

I now have a question for you. Have you reached a conclusion? From your perspective, is God only a myth, or a legend, or the product of wishful thinking? Or is he a divine reality who can change your life forever?

If you already considered yourself a Christian before picking up this book—is your faith now more strongly grounded?

Lining Up the Evidence

John Lennox is a mathematics professor at Oxford University; he's also a committed Christian who has debated several leading atheists. In these debates, he often insists that Christian faith is *not* a leap in the dark. He says that what Jesus wants from us is a faith that's more solid than that. "The kind of faith he is looking for," Lennox says, "is evidenced-based faith."

I believe this book has laid out convincing evidence that Christianity is firmly rooted in reality. Let's take a moment to review the issues we've investigated.

1. *The cosmos requires a creator.* Virtually all scientists now agree that the universe and physical time itself had a *beginning* at some point in the past. This seems logical. It looks true that whatever begins to exist must have a cause; therefore, the universe must have a cause behind it. A supernatural cause cannot easily be ruled out. In fact, the best explanation is a personal creator.

2. *The universe needs a fine-tuner.* Many of the most exciting discoveries of modern science have to do with how the universe operates. The numbers behind all this are calibrated with mind-boggling precision so that life can exist. This could hardly be by chance. The physical laws of the universe are so finely tuned that it defies any such explanation. Rather, all this points to a creator.

We can infer several things about this creator. He must exist *apart from* his creation, and *before* it was created. He must therefore be immaterial or spirit, and also timeless or eternal. He must be powerful, given the immense energy needed for the Big Bang. He must be smart, given the precision behind the creation event. And he must be personal, because a decision had to be made to create. Given the beautiful complexity of the universe and life itself, he must be highly creative. He must be caring, because he so purposefully crafted the human habitat. And the principle that we shouldn't multiply causes beyond what's necessary to explain an effect suggests there would be just one creator.

All those qualities happen to match the description of the God of Christianity. This rules out polytheism (belief in many gods) and also pantheism (which says everything is god).

Meanwhile, scientists in general have not embraced the idea of an infinite number of other universes. This idea is untestable and lacks any physical evidence. Prominent German physicist Sabine Hossenfelder, an agnostic, branded this theory "a waste of time" from a scientific perspective.

3. *Our DNA demands a designer.* Our DNA contains a vast storehouse of highly specific information. It comes in the form of a four-letter chemical alphabet that spells out the precise assembly instructions for all the proteins that make up our bodies. We can easily rule out chance or blind evolutionary forces as the explanation for this phenomenon, because information *always* has an intelligence behind it.

4. *Easter showed that Jesus is God.* In many ways during his days on earth, Jesus made divine claims about himself. After he died, he then rose from the dead on the third day—which strongly suggests that he told the truth about himself.

The fact of his resurrection is well supported by the historical record. This record includes significant evidence from eyewitnesses to the resurrected Jesus. Even opponents of Jesus implicitly admitted that his tomb was empty on the first Easter morning. This resurrection event is also supported by ancient sources outside the New Testament.

5. *Many people have reported personal experiences with God.* Throughout history, people have reported having dramatic and transformative personal experiences that they can only explain as coming from God. These include information received in dreams, with the information later verified by persons who could not otherwise have known it. Some of the most astounding experiences with God come in the form of miraculous answers to prayer.

6. *Which God is real?* When we reason through the grids of truth, worldviews, theism, revelation, resurrection, and the gospel—we're able to rule out atheism and pantheism as valid worldviews. We land on theism—and finally on Christianity—as being the best-supported option.

Christianity also matches the so-called moral argument for God's existence: If objective moral values are real, then God exists. We can identify objective moral values that are universally binding on all people at all times (whether they fully follow them or not). Since these values exist, we can logically conclude that God exists.

7. *Some have other objections.* For many people, there are other weighty questions to be considered. Two of the biggest objections to belief in God are these: the existence of suffering in the world, and God's apparent hiddenness. In the end, neither of those obstacles can reasonably overcome the other evidence that persuasively points toward the veracity of Christianity.

A Fallout from Atheism

When I was an atheist, I realized I would need to do more than raise random objections in order to cripple Christianity. I would have to come up with a complete alternative to theism that would better accommodate all the facts listed above. But the only hypothesis that explains them all is this: There's a divine creator whose unique Son is Jesus of Nazareth.

The evidence for God's existence—and for Christianity—is compelling. However, it is ultimately unsatisfying just to know a bunch of information *about* God. We need to personally meet and experience him.

That's why the quest for the real God must not end in the world of factual evidence, logical reasoning, philosophy, and science—even though the search can begin there. If God is real, then ultimately the only appropriate response is for us to seek and enjoy a personal relationship with him—a relationship that has no ending.

When I was an atheist, I came to understand that disbelief in God is in a real sense a dead end. It offers no transcendent meaning for life and no hope for an existence beyond this world.

I also came to see that atheism is not supported by the evidence of science, philosophy, and history. After spending two years investigating faith issues, I came to realize that to continue in my spiritual skepticism, these are the things I would need to believe:

Nothing produces everything.
Randomness produces fine-tuning.

When I was an atheist, I realized I would need to do more than raise random objections in order to cripple Christianity. I would have to come up with a complete alternative to theism that would better accommodate all the facts. But the only hypothesis that explains them all is this: There's a divine creator whose unique Son is Jesus of Nazareth.

Nonlife produces life.

Chaos produces information.

Unconsciousness produces consciousness.

Nonreason produces reason.

What's more, I would need to ignore the compelling data that supports the resurrection of Jesus as an actual event of history.

Honestly, I didn't have enough faith to continue to be an atheist.

Deciding God Is Real

Ultimately, faith isn't about having perfect and complete answers to every possible spiritual issue. After all, we don't demand that level of conclusive proof in any other arena of life. But we *do* have plenty evidence about God on which to act. And that's the ultimate issue.

Faith is about a choice, a step of the will, a decision to want to know God personally. It's humbly and vulnerably saying (as a man once said to Jesus, in Mark 9:24), "I believe. Please help me with my unbelief!"

God reveals himself to those who want to know him. I think that deep inside us all, either we truly want to believe, or we truly *don't* want to believe.

If your heart is one that truly desires to believe—there's encouraging news for you from both the Old and New Testaments:

"You will seek me and find me when you seek me with all your heart" (Jeremiah 29:13).

"God . . . rewards those who earnestly seek him" (Hebrews 11:6).

If you wholeheartedly seek God—you *will* find him.

In my own search, I was thankful that I didn't have to throw out my intellect to become a Christian. But I *did* have to overcome my pride. I had to drive a stake through my egoism and my arrogance. I had to push past my self-interest and self-glory that were keeping my heart shut tight from God.

What do I want? That was the big issue. Did I want to know God personally? Did I want release from guilt, plus the freedom to live the way God designed me to live? Did I want to pursue his purposes for my life? Did I want to tap into his power for daily living? Did I want to commune with him in this life and for eternity?

If so—I had plenty evidence as a basis for deciding to say yes to him.

So that's what I did on the afternoon of November 8, 1981. In effect, I declared to God, "You win."

Some people report having a rush of emotion at a moment like that. For me, it was different. *I felt the rush of reason.*

I wasn't sure what to do next, until my wife pointed out a Bible verse that clearly explained it. It's John 1:12—and I've emphasized here the key words: "Yet to all who did *receive* him, to those who *believed* in his name, he gave the right to *become* children of God."

Right there is the formula of faith: *Believe* + *Receive* = *Become.*

I *believed*, based on the evidence, that God is real and that Jesus is his unique Son.

So I *received* his forgiveness through a heartfelt prayer. In that prayer, I confessed my sinful behavior. And I acknowledged my desire to make a turn in life, in order to walk on God's path.

And with that, I *became* a child of God—for eternity.

As a result, over time God transformed my character, my morality, my values, my worldview, my attitudes, my priorities, and my relationships—all for the better.

Decision Time

So what's *your* conclusion? Which pathway is the evidence taking you down? Are you convinced God is real? Are you ready to personally meet and experience him through Jesus?

Or do you still need more evidence?

If you're uncertain about which direction to go, I suggest asking the God you're not sure exists to show himself to you. Ask him to do this through nature, through Scripture, and through any other way he chooses. You may want to repeat this twenty-word prayer: "God, if you open my eyes to who you really are—then I will open my life fully to you."

Once the evidence is in, it's time to decide. If you conclude that God is real, take the step I did by offering a heartfelt prayer of repentance and faith to receive his free gift of forgiveness and eternal life. Maybe it's time for you to pray along these lines:

> *Jesus, right now, as best I can, I do believe that you are the Son of God. You proved it by returning from the dead. And I admit the obvious, which is I am a sinner. I confess this and turn from my wrong beliefs and actions. In an attitude of repentance and faith, I receive your free gift of forgiveness and eternal life. Please fill me with your Holy Spirit and help me live the kind of life that you want me to live—because from this moment on, I am yours.*

If you'll do this, the greatest adventure of your life will begin. You become a follower of the One who conquered death and the grave. Over time you'll discover, as I have, that Jesus is the most glorious, the most beautiful, the most brilliant, the most loving, the most gracious, and the most forgiving Being in existence. He's kind, he's gentle, he's strong, he's encouraging, he's patient, he's pure, he's joyful—and above all else, he's *real*.

That, my friend, changes everything.

ADDITIONAL RELEVANT COMMENTS FROM SERIOUS THINKERS

Fazale Rana, who earned his doctorate in chemistry with an emphasis on biochemistry:

The harmony between the Bible's account of the origin of life and nature's record provides powerful evidence for the validity of the Christian faith.

—Fazale Rana, "Origin-of-Life Predictions Face Off: Evolution vs. Biblical Creation," Reasons to Believe, March 31, 2001, https://reasons.org/explore/publications/rtb-101/origin-of-life-predictions-face-off-evolution-vs-biblical-creation.

Colin McGinn, philosopher:

How did evolution convert the water of biological tissue into the wine of consciousness? Consciousness seems like a radical novelty in the universe, not prefigured by the after-effects of the Big Bang, so how did it contrive to spring into being from what preceded it?

—Colin McGinn, *The Mysterious Flame: Conscious Minds in a Material World* (New York: Basic Books, 1999), 13–14.

***

Sharon Dirckx, Cambridge-trained neuroscientist:

The unembodied mind of God, which has always existed, gave rise to everything else. The Bible also says that human beings were made in God's image. Consequently, it makes sense to say that because God has a mind, we have a mind; because God thinks, we think; because God is conscious, so are we. . . .

If the materialistic narrative is all there is, then we can throw meaning, purpose, and significance out the window. We're a blip on the landscape. The cosmos is billions of years old, and we appear in the last millisecond. We are utterly meaningless. . . .

The reason all of us have a longing for eternity is that, indeed, we were made by God to live forever. God is relational, existing from eternity past as the Trinity. And so like him, we are relational beings. This means we can interact personally with God. He is someone to be encountered. He is a first-person experience, not a third-person observation.

—As interviewed by Lee Strobel in *The Case for Heaven: A Journalist Investigates Evidence for Life after Death* (Grand Rapids: Zondervan, 2021), 43-44.

***

J. P. Moreland, professor of philosophy, Talbot School of Theology, Biola University, and coauthor of *The Substance of Consciousness*:

Consciousness cannot be reduced merely to the physical brain. This means the atheist creation story is inadequate and false. And yet there is an alternative explanation that makes sense of all the evidence: Our consciousness came from a greater Consciousness.

—As interviewed by Lee Strobel in *The Case for a Creator: A Journalist Investigates Scientific Evidence That Points toward God* (Grand Rapids: Zondervan, 2004), 270.

John A. O'Keefe of NASA, Harvard-trained astrophysicist, considered "the godfather of modern astrogeology," and recipient of the Goddard Space Flight Center's highest award:

If the universe had not been made with the most exacting precision we could never have come into existence. It is my view that these circumstances indicate the universe was created for man to live in.

—As quoted in Robert Jastrow, *God and the Astronomers*, 2nd ed. (New York: Norton, 1992), 118.

George Sim Johnson, science writer:

Human DNA contains more organized information than the *Encyclopedia Britannica*. If the full text of the encyclopedia were to arrive in computer code from outer space, most people would regard this as proof of the existence of extraterrestrial intelligence. But when seen in nature, it is explained as the workings of random forces.

—George Sim Johnson, "Did Darwin Get It Right?" *Wall Street Journal*, October 15, 1999.

Blaise Pascal, seventeenth-century French philosopher:

The Christian's God does not consist merely of a God who is the author of mathematical truths, but the God of Abraham, Isaac, and Jacob. The God of the Christians is a God of love and consolation: he is a God who fills the soul and heart of those whom he possesses: he is a God who makes them inwardly aware of their wretchedness and his infinite mercy: who unites himself with them in the depths of their soul: who fills it with humility, joy, confidence, and love: who makes them incapable of having any other end but him.

—Blaise Pascal, *Pensées*, trans. W. F. Trotter (Overland Park, KS: Digireads, 2018), 121.

Staks Rosch, writer for SkepticInk.com, the *HuffPost*, and others:

Depression is a serious problem in the greater atheist community and far too often, that depression has led to suicide. This is something many of my fellow atheists often don't like to admit, but it is true.

—Staks Rosch, "Atheism Has a Suicide Problem," *HuffPost*, December 8, 2017, www.huffpost.com/entry/atheism-has-a-suicide-problem_b_5a2a902ee4b022ec613b812b.

***

W. Mark Lanier, prominent attorney and founder of the Lanier Theological Library in Houston, author of *Atheism on Trial*; here he outlines a worldview based on a biblical God:

1. Outside of the universe is an infinite, personal, and moral 'God' or Being responsible for the universe's existence.

2. Humans are unique among living beings, because people bear an imprint (image) of God, by being both moral and personal.

3. Humans exist to be in a personal relationship with God.

4. Humans do not measure up fully to God's morality, making a truly harmonious relationship impossible by itself.

5. Only God can provide a just mechanism to establish that personal relationship, all while maintaining and not compromising God's just and moral character. Deduction: 'Right' and 'wrong' have meaning, whether people accept it or not. They are defined by and rooted in the morality of God. Implications: People are not mere space dust. People have dignity and honor as beings bearing the image of God.

—W. Mark Lanier, *Atheism on Trial: A Lawyer Examines the Case for Unbelief* (Downers Grove, IL: InterVarsity, 2022), 59.

Nancy R. Pearcey, university professor, bestselling author, and former agnostic:

Christianity offers a genuine alternative to an empty, pointless cosmos. It says that we are not alone, that the universe is meaningful, that we do have intrinsic value, that sexuality has its own purpose or *telos*, that human community is real, and that there is objective truth, goodness, and beauty. Most of all, we are not the products of mindless chance but the creation of a loving Creator.

—Nancy R. Pearcey, *Love Thy Body: Answering Hard Questions about Life and Sexuality*, rev. ed. (Grand Rapids: Baker, 2019), 256.

***

Paul Copan, professor of philosophy and ethics, Palm Beach Atlantic University (Florida), and author of *Is God a Vindictive Bully?* and *Loving Wisdom*:

The moral argument is, in my estimation, the most powerful argument for God, and I have seen plenty of intellectual and spiritual seekers find God because of it.

—Personal email to author, dated December 12, 2022.

T. M. Luhrmann, Oxford-trained anthropologist:

If you could believe in God, why wouldn't you? There is good evidence that those who believe in a loving God have happier lives. Loneliness is bad for people in many different ways . . . and we know that people who believe in God are less lonely. . . . We know that those who go to church live longer and in greater health. . . . This God loves unconditionally; he forgives freely; he brings joy. Why would one not believe?

—T. M. Luhrmann, *When God Talks: Understanding the American Evangelical Relationship with God* (New York: Knopf, 2012), xvi.

***

Mary Jo Sharp, professor of apologetics at Houston Christian University, and founder of Confident Christianity Ministries:

As I explored the atheist arguments, they were not convincing, nor did they have any grounding for substantive and meaningful hope. I couldn't go back to atheism after studying the arguments for and against God's existence. It would have been intellectually dishonest.

—For more on Mary Jo Sharp's journey, see her *Why I Still Believe: A Former Atheist's Reckoning with the Bad Reputation Christians Give a Good God* (Grand Rapids: Zondervan, 2019).

FOR YOUR FURTHER INVESTIGATION

From Lee Strobel

The Case for a Creator: A Journalist Investigates Scientific Evidence That Points Toward God (Zondervan, 2004).

The Case for Christ: A Journalist's Personal Investigation of the Evidence for Jesus, updated and expanded edition (Zondervan, 2016).

The Case for Faith: A Journalist Investigates the Toughest Objections to Christianity, updated and expanded edition (Zondervan, 2021).

The Case for Grace: A Journalist Explores the Evidence of Transformed Lives (Zondervan, 2015).

In Defense of Jesus: Investigating Attacks on the Identity of Christ (Zondervan, 2007).

Seeing the Supernatural: Investigating Angels, Demons, Mystical Dreams, Near-Death Encounters, and Other Mysteries of the Unseen World (Zondervan, 2025).

Other Authors Highlighted in This Book

From William Lane Craig:

(and coauthor Quentin Smith) *Theism, Atheism, and Big Bang Cosmology* (Oxford University Press, 1993).

The Kalam Cosmological Argument (Wipf and Stock, 2000).

Reasonable Faith: Christian Truth and Apologetics, third edition (Crossway, 2008).

The Son Rises: Historical Evidence for the Resurrection of Jesus (Wipf and Stock, 2000).

From Douglas Groothuis:

Christian Apologetics: A Comprehensive Case for Biblical Faith (IVP Academic, 2016).

World Religion in Seven Sentences: A Small Introduction to a Vast Topic (IVP Academic, 2023).

From Peter Kreeft:

Making Sense out of Suffering (Servant, 1986).

From Michael R. Licona:

(and coauthor Gary R. Habermas) *The Case for the Resurrection of Jesus* (Kregel, 2004).

The Resurrection of Jesus: A New Historiographical Approach (IVP Academic, 2010).

From Chad Meister:

Evil: A Guide for the Perplexed, second edition (Bloomsbury Academic, 2018).

From Stephen C. Meyer:

Darwin's Doubt: The Explosive Origin of Animal Life and the Case for Intelligent Design (HarperOne, 2014).

Return of the God Hypothesis: Three Scientific Discoveries That Reveal the Mind Behind the Universe (HarperOne, 2021).

Signature in the Cell: DNA and the Evidence for Intelligent Design (HarperOne, 2010).

From Kenneth Samples:

Christianity Cross-Examined: Is It Rational, Relevant, and Good? (RTB Press, 2021).

God Among Sages: Why Jesus Is Not Just Another Religious Leader (Baker, 2017).

(and coauthor Mark Perez) *Clear Thinking in a Messy World: A Christian Guide to Logic, Reason, and Cognitive Bias* (RTB Press, 2024).

Resources by Other Authors

Atheism on Trial: A Lawyer Examines the Case for Unbelief, W. Mark Lanier (InterVarsity, 2022).

Body of Proof: The 7 Best Reasons to Believe in the Resurrection of Jesus—and Why It Matters Today, Jeremiah Johnston (Bethany House, 2023).

Broken Planet: If There's a God, Then Why Are There Natural Disasters and Diseases?, Sharon Dirckx (IVP, 2023).

Can We Still Believe the Bible? An Evangelical Engagement with Contemporary Questions, Craig L. Blomberg (Brazos, 2014).

Can We Trust the Gospels? Investigating the Reliability of Matthew, Mark, Luke, and John, Mark D. Roberts (Crossway, 2007).

Can We Trust the Gospels?, Peter J. Williams (Crossway, 2018).

Cold-Case Christianity: A Homicide Detective Investigates the Claims of the Gospel, J. Warner Wallace (Cook, 2013).

Darwin Strikes Back: Defending the Science of Intelligent Design, Thomas Woodward (Baker, 2006).

Designed to the Core, Hugh Ross (RTB Press, 2022).

Divine Hiddenness: New Essays, Daniel Howard-Snyder and Paul K. Moser, eds. (Cambridge University Press, 2001).

Escaping the Beginning? Confronting Challenges to the Universe's Origin, Jeff Zweerink (RTB Press, 2019).

The Evidential Force of Religious Experience, Caroline Franks Davis (Clarendon, 1989).

Evil and the Justice of God, N. T. Wright (InterVarsity, 2013).

The Existence of God, second edition, Richard Swinburne (Clarendon, 2004).

A Fortunate Universe: Life in a Finely Tuned Cosmos, Geraint F. Lewis and Luke A. Barnes (Cambridge University Press, 2016).

God's Crime Scene: A Cold-Case Detective Examines the Evidence for a Divinely Created Universe, J. Warner Wallace (David C. Cook, 2015).

Good God: The Theistic Foundations of Morality, David Baggett and Jerry Walls (Oxford University Press, 2011).

The Hiddenness of God, reprint edition, Michael C. Rea (Oxford University Press, 2021).

If God, Why Evil? A New Way to Think About the Question, Norman L. Geisler (Bethany House, 2011).

Improbable Planet: How Earth Became Humanity's Home, Hugh Ross (Baker, 2016).

In Defense of the Bible: A Comprehensive Apologetic for the Authority of Scripture, Steven B. Cowan and Terry L. Wilder, eds. (B&H Academic, 2013).

Jesus' Resurrection: Fact or Figment? A Debate Between William Lane Craig and Gerd Lüdemann, Paul Copan and Ronald K. Tacelli, eds. (IVP Academic, 2000).

Mere Creation: Science, Faith and Intelligent Design, William A. Dembski, ed. (InterVarsity, 1998).

The Miracle of Man: The Fine Tuning of Nature for Human Existence, Michael Denton (Discovery Institute Press, 2022).

The Morals of the Story: Good News About a Good God, David Baggett and Marybeth Baggett (IVP Academic, 2018).

Naming the Elephant: Worldview as a Concept, James W. Sire (InterVarsity, 2004).

The Privileged Planet: How Our Place in the Cosmos Is Designed for Discovery, Guillermo Gonzalez and Jay W. Richards (Regnery, 2004).

The Problem of Pain, reprint edition, C. S. Lewis (HarperCollins, 2001).

Putting Jesus in His Place: The Case for the Deity of Christ, Robert M. Bowman Jr. and J. Ed Komoszewski (Kregel, 2007).

Questioning the Bible: 11 Major Challenges to the Bible's Authority, Jonathan Morrow (Moody, 2014).

Rare Earth: Why Complex Life Is Uncommon in the Universe, Peter D. Ward and Donald Brownlee (Copernicus, 2000).

The Rationality of Theism, Paul Copan and Paul K. Moser, eds. (Routledge, 2003).

The Reason Why: Faith Makes Sense, Mark Mittelberg (Tyndale, 2011).

Relativism: Feet Firmly Planted in Mid-Air, Francis J. Beckwith and Gregory Koukl (Baker, 1998).

Religions on Trial: A Lawyer Examines Buddhism, Hinduism, Islam, and More, W. Mark Lanier (InterVarsity, 2023).

Religious Experience and the Knowledge of God: The Evidential Force of Divine Encounters, Harold A. Netland (Baker Academic, 2022).

The Resurrection of God Incarnate, Richard Swinburne (Clarendon, 2003).

The Resurrection of the Son of God, N. T. Wright (Fortress Press, 2003).

Signposts to God: How Modern Physics and Astronomy Point the Way to Belief, Peter Bussey (IVP Academic, 2016).

Simply Good News: Why the Gospel Is News and What Makes It Good, N. T. Wright (HarperOne, 2015).

Truth in a Culture of Doubt: Engaging Skeptical Challenges to the Bible, Andreas J. Köstenberger, Darrell L. Bock, and Josh D. Chatraw (B&H, 2014).

Understanding the Times: A Survey of Competing Worldviews, Jeff Myers and David A. Noebel (David C. Cook, 2015).

Walking with God Through Pain and Suffering, Timothy Keller (Penguin, 2015).

Where Is God in All the Suffering?, Amy Orr-Ewing (Good Book, 2020).

Where Is God When Bad Things Happen? Finding Solace in Times of Trouble, Luis Palau (Doubleday, 1999).

Where Is God? Divine Absence in the Hebrew Bible, Joel S. Burnett (Fortress Press, 2010).

Why Does God Allow Evil? Compelling Answers for Life's Toughest Questions, Clay Jones (Harvest House, 2017).

Why the Universe Is the Way It Is, Hugh Ross (Baker, 2008).

Why? Looking at God, Evil, and Personal Suffering, Sharon Dirckx (InterVarsity, 2021).

Worldviews in Conflict: Choosing Christianity in a World of Ideas, Ronald H. Nash (Zondervan, 1992).

Your Designed Body, Steve Laufmann and Howard Glicksman (Discovery Institute Press, 2022).

GUIDE FOR REFLECTION AND GROUP DISCUSSION

For your own deeper reflection—or to help in discussing this book in a group with others—I've put together the following questions that I hope will stimulate your thinking.

This is *not* a Bible study. Rather, it's designed simply to aid you in further exploring the evidence, arguments, and perspectives presented in this book.

Wherever you find yourself on your spiritual journey, I hope this guide will help you analyze, understand, and personalize the points made by the experts I interviewed on the all-important topic of *Is God real?*

Introduction—How My Search Began

1. How would you describe your current perspective on Christianity?

2. What question would you ask about God if you knew he would give you an answer right now? What is it that motivates you to want him to answer that one for you?

3. If you were to tell the story of your own spiritual journey in just one paragraph, what would you say?

4. How different do you think the world would look if *everyone* lived as if God is *not* real?

5. Philosopher Douglas Groothuis has said, "We all experience a deep sense of yearning or longing for something that the present natural world cannot fulfill—something transcendently glorious." How true is that for you?

6. In prayer (while being certain that God is listening), express what you most want to communicate to him at this time.

Chapter 1—The Cosmos Requires a Creator

1. In your opinion, what is the strongest piece of evidence presented in this chapter?

2. What questions or doubts come to your mind about any of the evidence presented in this chapter?

3. What emotions have you felt in looking up into a star-filled night sky, or upon a beautiful sunlit scene in nature (in the mountains, beside the ocean—wherever)? How would you describe what it is inside you that prompted those emotions?

4. To what degree would you expect a scientist's personal worldview to affect his or her willingness to follow the evidence wherever it leads?

5. How convincing is the first premise of the kalam cosmological argument—that whatever begins to exist has a cause behind it? Can you conceive of anything that has come into existence *without* some sort of cause?

6. The second premise of the kalam argument states that the universe began to exist. Do you think the evidence from mathematics and science sufficiently supports the claim that the universe had a beginning at some point in the past? Why or why not?

7. The kalam argument states that if those first two premises are true, then it's logical to conclude that *the universe has a cause.* Can you think of any alternative theory that would support a different conclusion?

8. How persuaded are you that the cause of the universe must be *personal*? If that's true, what bearing does that have on the way you view your life and the world around you?

9. In your own understanding, is it possible for something to come from nothing? Why or why not?

Chapter 2—The Universe Needs a Fine-Tuner

1. In your opinion, what is the strongest piece of evidence presented in this chapter?

2. What questions or doubts come to your mind about any of the evidence presented in this chapter?

3. What impresses you most about the fine-tuning of the universe, as discussed in this chapter?

4. Do you think it's possible that the fine-tuning we see in the universe could be the result of random chance? Why or why not?

5. Some scientists believe that a valid "Theory of Everything" might someday be discovered, and this could fully explain in a natural way the fine-tuning of the universe. Other scientists believe that this would actually be stronger evidence for a creator. Which position do you find most convincing, and why?

6. Do you believe that ours is the only universe in existence, or can you imagine that some other universes might also exist? What specific evidence prompts your belief? If multiple universes *do* exist—then in your thinking, does that reinforce the idea of intelligent design behind creation?

7. What are your thoughts in response to this proposed statement: "The universe was created for human beings to live in"? Assuming that this is true—what are some reasons why God might have been motivated to pursue this plan? And how would that relate to you personally?

Chapter 3—Our DNA Demands a Designer

1. In your opinion, what is the strongest piece of evidence presented in this chapter?

2. What questions or doubts come to your mind about any of the evidence presented in this chapter?

3. While scientists are virtually unanimous in ruling out random chance for the origin of life, this theory is still common in the general population. Especially from what you understand about the amount of organized information contained in human DNA—how likely does it seem that this could be explained as the result of random forces?

4. In your science classes at school, have you come across the idea that life emerged somehow from a "prebiotic soup" of chemicals on the primitive Earth? If so, how do you react to the lack of any evidence that this ever existed?.

5. The theory that life is intelligently designed sometimes generates heated controversy. Do you personally feel any kind of emotional resistance to the idea that intelligent design is behind all life in the universe? If so, why do you think that is?

Chapter 4—Easter Showed That Jesus Is God

1. In your opinion, what is the strongest piece of evidence presented in this chapter?

2. What questions or doubts come to your mind about any of the evidence presented in this chapter?

3. Theologians believe that without the resurrection of Jesus, there could be no Christianity. The apostle Paul wrote (in 1 Corinthians 15:17) that if Jesus had not risen from the dead, "your faith is futile." Why would that be so? Why is Christ's resurrection so important for Christians?

4. If you were a historian investigating the resurrection of Jesus, what evidence would you look for? What facts from history would convince you that Jesus rose from the dead?

5. The first of the "minimal facts" mentioned by Michael Licona in this chapter is that Jesus was killed by crucifixion. He has said that Jesus's death on the cross is "as solid as anything in ancient history." How solid does his evidence appear to you?

6. Licona's second "minimal fact" is that the disciples believed that Jesus rose and appeared to them. He lists several historical sources in support of that conclusion.

How would you evaluate the credibility of those sources? Which source did you find most convincing?

7. If you had known Jesus in his childhood and early youth (as his brother James did), what would it take to later convince you that he was the Son of God?

8. Licona provides various reasons for believing the tomb of Jesus was empty. Are his points enough to convince you that Jesus's tomb was indeed empty that first Easter morning? Why or why not?

9. Are you convinced by what you've seen in this chapter that Jesus did indeed rise from the dead, thus proving that he's the unique Son of God? Why or why not? And what does your conclusion mean for how you live your life?

Chapter 5—Experiencing God

1. In your opinion, what is the strongest piece of evidence presented in this chapter?

2. What questions or doubts come to your mind about any of the evidence presented in this chapter?

3. Have you had an experience in your life that you can explain as only the work of God? If so, describe the circumstances. How did this incident influence your faith, or your openness to faith?

4. What do you think are the best ways to evaluate these kinds of experiences?

5. It's understandable that a spiritual experience would have an impact on the person going through it. But when you hear about experiences that other people went through—how does that affect you? Do you tend to be skeptical? Or is it easy for you to accept what they describe as being true?

6. How would you respond to a skeptic who claims that all religious experiences are somehow fake?

7. The Bible teaches that followers of Christ will experience God in various ways—through his comfort, his guidance, his discipline, his peace, and so forth. Have

you experienced any of these benefits? If so, describe the situation. What made you confident that this was God's activity or help on your behalf?

8. Douglas Groothuis cautions us in this chapter that an experience from God isn't enough, by itself, to establish that God exists; he says we should consider other kinds of evidence as well. Think about some of the evidence for God you've read so far in this book. What do you find most persuasive?

Chapter 6—Which God Is Real?

1. In your opinion, what is the strongest piece of evidence presented in this chapter?

2. What questions or doubts come to your mind about any of the evidence presented in this chapter?

3. As you began reading this chapter, in which of the following ways would you have classified yourself:

   a. hardcore skeptic
   b. moderate skeptic
   c. spiritually neutral person
   d. spiritual seeker
   e. believer in Christ
   f. strong and confident Christian

   Did this chapter change where you fit in this list? If so, in what way?

4. In this chapter, Chad Meister speaks of going through a period of doubting Christianity after he encountered credible people of other religions. Have you ever doubted your faith? What caused this? How did you process that experience? Did you come to any resolution?

5. Does Meister's apologetics pyramid make sense to you? Do you believe it covers the essential issues that need to be investigated? Which level of the pyramid was the most important for you and why?

6. Pontius Pilate famously asked, "What is truth?" How would you answer him? Is your answer different now from what it would have been before you read this chapter?

7. The Qur'an (the scriptures of the religion of Islam) and the Bible make conflicting claims. If you were confronted with some of these, how would you go about comparing and evaluating the differences? How would you go about deciding which one was right?

8. If Jesus was resurrected, it would be a miracle—but miracles are possible if God exists. Philosopher Richard Purtill has described a miracle as an event brought about by the power of God that is a temporary exception to the ordinary course of nature, for the purpose of showing that God has acted in history.

   Think carefully about the different parts of this definition. Does it make sense to you? Have you had an experience in your life that you can only describe as a miracle—and which seems in line with that definition above? If so, what happened? How did it affect you?

9. The top level of Meister's pyramid is the gospel. If someone asked you why Jesus died for our sins, what would you say to them?

Chapter 7—Challenge #1: If God Is Real, Why Is There Suffering?

1. Have you personally encountered pain or suffering in your life that made you question the existence of a loving God? What were the circumstances? What emotions did you encounter? What impact did this have on your spiritual outlook, or in your faith journey? What impact does it still have?

2. Have you been sincerely seeking God? If so, in what ways? What progress have you made? How confident are you that you will find God in the end?

3. Peter Kreeft makes the comment that the existence of evil is evidence *for* God. Do you find his reasons for this credible? Why or why not?

4. Kreeft raises this question: "How is it possible that more than 90 percent of all the human beings who have ever lived—usually in far more painful circumstances than we—could believe in God?" How would you answer him?

5. Kreeft says that God took the very worst thing that could ever happen in the universe (the death of the Son of God) and turned it into the very best thing that has ever happened (opening up heaven and God's kingdom to all who follow him). Do you find this helpful in considering the

suffering in your own life? Do you think other people who suffer (perhaps much more than you have suffered) would find this helpful?

6. Think about experiences you've gone through that were especially difficult, challenging, or painful. Did going through these experiences help you to learn and grow and mature as a person? If so, in what ways?

7. How did this chapter influence your overall viewpoint about suffering?

8. Do you believe that a person can logically conclude that God exists and still not have a fully satisfactory answer for why he allows suffering?

Chapter 8—Challenge #2: If God Is Real, Why Is He So Hidden?

1. Have you ever felt frustrated or exasperated because God has been silent when you've wanted to hear more personally from him? If so, what were the circumstances?

2. If God today made himself more apparent to everyone everywhere, how do you think people would respond?

3. In the Bible, we're told in Romans 1 that there is adequate evidence in nature for people to recognize that God exists. However, we tend to suppress this truth and forget about God. Why do you think we have that tendency?

4. Could the apparent hiddenness of God actually have positive effects on some people? How so? Can you think of some circumstances in your own life in which this might be true?

5. When do you sense God's hiddenness the most?

Conclusion—Your Own Encounter with the Real God

1. How has your faith in God—or lack of it—affected your everyday life? Can you see a specific impact on your physical, emotional, or psychological health? How so?

2. This conclusion to the book lists the following as required beliefs for someone who wants to continue in atheism:

   - Nothing produces everything.
   - Randomness produces fine-tuning.
   - Nonlife produces life.
   - Chaos produces information.
   - Unconsciousness produces consciousness.
   - Nonreason produces reason.

   Do you think this list is a fair assessment of what atheism involves? Which of these would be the hardest for you to believe, and why? And which might be the easiest to believe, and why?

3. How fully do you believe that God will indeed reveal himself to the person who truly wants to know him?

4. How deep is your own desire to know God?

5. What is your biggest desire? Is it bigger than your desire to know God?

6. From John 1:12 comes this formula for faith: *Believe + Receive = Become.* If you don't yet believe that God is real and that Jesus is his unique Son—why not pray the seeker's prayer: "God, if you open my eyes to who you really are, then I will open my life fully to you."

7. What additional steps do you plan to take in your quest for spiritual answers? How do you plan to continue pursuing the truth about God? (Two ideas: read a book from the recommended resources list, and attend a good local church.)

8. If you believe that God is real and Jesus is his Son who died for your sins, have you received his free gift of forgiveness and eternal life? If so, describe what happened. Was your experience more like a rush of emotion, or a rush of reason?

   If you haven't taken that step, why not do it right now in a prayer of repentance and faith? And if you take that step to receive God's grace—who will be the first person you tell, and why?

MEET LEE STROBEL

Atheist-turned-Christian Lee Strobel, the former award-winning legal editor of the *Chicago Tribune*, is a *New York Times* bestselling author of more than forty books and curricula that have sold eighteen million copies in total. His books have received more than 25,000 five-star reviews on Amazon and have been translated into forty languages.

Lee has been described in *The Washington Post* as "one of the evangelical community's most popular apologists." He was educated at the University of Missouri (where he received a bachelor of journalism degree) and Yale Law School (where he earned a master's degree in studies in law). He was a journalist for fourteen years at the *Chicago Tribune* and other newspapers, winning Illinois's highest honors for both investigative reporting and public service journalism from United Press International.

After probing the evidence for Jesus for nearly two years, Lee became a Christian in 1981. He subsequently became a teaching pastor at three of America's largest churches and hosted the weekly national network TV program *Faith*

Under Fire. In addition, he taught First Amendment law at Roosevelt University and was a professor of Christian thought at Houston Baptist University.

In 2017, Lee's spiritual journey was depicted in an award-winning motion picture, *The Case for Christ*. Lee won national awards for his books *The Case for Christ*, *The Case for Faith*, *The Case for a Creator*, and *The Case for Grace*. His most recent books are *The Case for Miracles*, *The Case for Heaven*, *Is God Real?* and *Seeing the Supernatural*, which debuted on the *New York Times* bestsellers list.

Lee and Leslie have been married for fifty-three years. Their daughter, Alison Morrow, is a novelist and homes-chooling expert, and their son, Kyle, is a professor of spiritual theology at the Talbot School of Theology at Biola University.

The Case for a Creator - Student Edition

A Journalist Investigates Scientific Evidence That Points Toward God

Lee Strobel with Jane Vogel

Does God really exist? Lee Strobel wasn't so sure. So, he decided to use his award-winning journalistic skills to investigate the creation story and prove once and for all if the claims about God the Creator are true. *The Case for a Creator Student Edition* adapts Strobel's bestselling book to present hard-hitting findings as well as Lee's journey from skepticism to belief in an easy-to-follow manner so you can make a decision about God for yourself. This student edition provides an apologetic look at Christian theology and philosophy for teens.

Pick up a copy at your favorite bookstore or online!

The Case for the Real Jesus - Student Edition

A Journalist Investigates Current Challenges to Christianity

Lee Strobel with Jane Vogel

There's proof a man named Jesus of Nazareth once walked the earth, but opinions on who he was vary widely. Was he really the Son of God, or was he a nice guy who did some positive things on earth, or was he possibly an unstable man? And how can you know for sure what is true and what is false when it comes to what you've read or been told? Lee Strobel decided to investigate the real, historical Jesus and gather irrefutable evidence on everything connected to him so you can discover the biblical truth for yourself.